WITHDRAWN

THE ART OF THE T'ANG POTTER

I LARGE HORSE. *Collection Count Cesare Cicogna, Milano (lift plate for details)*

MARIO PRODAN

THE ART OF THE T'ANG POTTER

with 154 illustrations including 34 plates in colour

A STUDIO BOOK

THE VIKING PRESS · NEW YORK

© THAMES AND HUDSON LTD 1960

PUBLISHED IN 1961 BY THE VIKING PRESS INC

LIBRARY OF CONGRESS CATALOG CARD NUMBER 61-8064

TEXT PRINTED BY BOSCH EN ZOON UTRECHT HOLLAND

MONOCHROME ILLUSTRATIONS PRINTED BY

BRAUN ET CIE MULHOUSE FRANCE

COLOUR ILLUSTRATIONS PRINTED BY

PARTRIDGE PRINTERS LTD LEEDS ENGLAND

COLOUR ENGRAVING BY GILCHRIST BROS LTD LEEDS ENGLAND

BOUND BY VAN RIJMENAM N.V. THE HAGUE HOLLAND

Contents

IN OUR TIME, when a long history of discovery and invention has jaded our sense of awe, it is perhaps difficult to imagine the happy wonder that descended on those of our ancestors who discovered that a clay object could be made solid and permanent by judicious exposure to fire. The discovery, stimulated by man's necessity, must have followed shortly after that of fire. Man's necessity includes, of course, those yearnings which have always gone beyond his material needs; so that the facile axiom that the mother of invention is necessity is only true if it is joined to another, that invention's father is the human spirit, that mysterious coercion which springs from man's imagination. Probably, once fire was invented it was immediately used to keep the dangerous beasts at bay, but equally probably the great invention was simultaneously employed to establish a rapport with the other world, with that dim void wherein dwelt the dark forces, no less real to the men of that age than their very material needs.

The first desire to produce something functional out of clay must have instantly been followed by this other urge to use the new skill to procure one more link with the supernatural. Modelled figures and animals could be placed upon the altar as homage along with vessels containing offerings. One can well imagine that the impulsion to self-expression, already at work in the creation of domestic vessels, was allowed even wider play in this new and wonderful pursuit of recreating things seen, until it achieved its greatest scope when man began to reproduce things seen not with the eye but with the imagination, the countless fantastic creatures portrayed in every very early civilisation.

It has been said that the advance of man towards his emancipation from nature is marked by the milestones of his discoveries and inventions. Every new knowledge gives him more strength, and strength, we know, banishes fear. If this is so, it is not difficult to imagine how, in time, man decided to make use of his new skill in order to emancipate himself from the terrors that beset his dreams: by substituting his clay reproductions for the men, women and beasts he had been wont to slaughter in order to propitiate the gods.

That this ethical jump, this passage from true to figurative sacrifice, did actually occur in China we have ample proof. Human remains kneaded into the earth that sealed the tombs disappear as earthenware statuettes begin to adorn the inside of the tombs – fierce pottery warriors wearing helmets not unlike those found on the very skulls of slaughtered body-guards: sculptured maidens whose clay draperies hide delicate bones exactly like the real ones found in the mud walls of the earlier tombs: figures of dogs, bullocks and horses in rich caparisons identical with those of the real animals sacrificed and buried with their princely but barbarian owners under the Altai. The savagery of the bigoted Shang warriors gradually gives way to the gentleness kindled in the princes by the mild philosophers of Chou. Enlightened dignitaries now commission their sacrificial material from master potters – from artists who, however, have not relinquished the religious awe that in China has always illuminated all traffic with the dead. The *lares* and *penates* are important: on the other side of the gate which separates life from death they have the ear of the gods of heaven and of the earth, of the almighty spirits who regulate rainfall, harvests, fertility and battles. This traffic, through the long period of its development, has become stiff with ritual. But ritual means order, and order civilisation.

In this order the person who had the gift of creating the objects so intimately connected with the rites, the potter, must have occupied a place of considerable importance. It has been supposed that the discovery of metal, too, can be credited to the potter, concerned as he was with the insinuation of earth into fire. Since bronze, that alloy, that has so enchanted the Chinese, was also used in the creation of sacrificial instruments and ritual vessels, its discovery would further have enhanced his status. And if it seems strange to us that such important people should have remained anonymous, that no potter-artist's name should appear in the annals or on the objects themselves, we shall see how this conforms to the Chinese manner, the only one to ensure an organic evolution of pottery-forms which attained full flower in the age with which we are here concerned.

Europe did not discover these fine ceramic works until long after it had become acquainted with what it considered Chinese Art. The East India Companies –

II · LADY FEEDING A BIRD. *41 cm. high. The type, if not the gentle occupation, leads us to believe that this particular substitute for human sacrifice is the portrait of a wife. Portliness in China, and in the T'ang period particularly, was regarded as a virtue in a person no longer very young, perhaps because it denoted a condition of emotional tranquillity, ever a Confucian ideal; or perhaps because the Chinese garment has always succeeded in transforming a person's abundance into stateliness. Even after Western fashions – from Persia, Kuchā and Turkey – put the traditional Chinese flowing robe into some eclipse, portly ladies went on wearing it; and portly gentlemen, too. A Chinese scholar has remarked that fat in a person is 'dignity where it emerges from the frame and comedy where it recedes'. The Chinese long gown has always enhanced the first and hidden the second.* Collection Dott. Alessandro Campilli, Rome

Portuguese, Dutch, English and French – began their trade in Chinese porcelain, lacquer and embroidery in the year 1600. These soldier-merchants introduced, along with their exotic wares, a vogue for Chinese decoration which found its way into the boudoir of Madame de Pompadour and through the workshops of Mr Thomas Chippendale into the antimacassared horror-chambers of our great-grandfathers.

The fine burial pieces which interest us were only discovered as late as the beginning of this century, accidentally, by Belgian and English industrialists who were bringing their technical pressure to bear on China, mainly in the field of railroad construction. How much the beauty of the objects they came across impressed these dour empire-builders it is difficult to say. But there is no doubt that the commercial possibilities presently became clear, if not to them, to their assistants and diggers; the Chinese have certainly never wanted for mercantile imagination. Soon pieces began to find their way to London where their importance was almost immediately recognised by connoisseurs and collectors.

A historical study of these initial contacts with the first objects to be dug out of China's earth might yield interesting conclusions and clear up many points. At any rate it is logical to assume that the reason why the first and most important labourers in this field of study were the English is because London was then already the most important art market in the world. Certainly no scholars have contributed more to our knowledge of China's artistic past than the English; and in ceramics, the field particularly dear to them, none has surpassed Hobson, David and Honey.

In a world being awakened to the romance of the past by the great archaeologists of the past century these finds could not fail to arouse great curiosity. But the severities of the dying Manchu rule and the tomb-respecting doctrines of Confucianism which it was trying desperately to uphold prohibited official digging. All theorising had, therefore, to be done in the dusty store rooms of museums, on

III   BOWL. *10½ cm. high. The base of this earthenware vessel clearly shows the typical fired clay of the whole range of the glazed and unglazed ware in these colour plates, though often the pinkish hue is absent. This is a footless receptacle fitting comfortably into the open hand – a holy man's begging bowl. The lug-holes were probably for a cord to pass through so that the bowl could be hung over the shoulder when it was not in use. Priests from the Lama Temple in Peking are often met on the streets holding bowls such as this and asking for alms to be placed into them.*   Collection Marchese G. Litta-Modignani, Capalbio

IV   TRIPOD BOWL. *21 cm. diameter. The discolouration in the centre of the bowl is iridescence brought about by contact with acids in the earth. The brilliance of the blue is unusual. In their pilgrimage through time the long, knifelike legs of the bronze chüeh – in turn a stylisation of the li of neolithic pottery – have become feet, as organically placed as the front legs on a Chinese pug.*   Collection Comm. Corrado Zingone, Rome

the testimony of material that was beginning to pour in from China thanks to the zeal of grave-robbers, dealers and foreign merchants.

Among these objects was a group of very fine bronze vessels known to date from the remote past – the fifteenth to the fourth century B.C. This dating had been arrived at mostly from Chinese texts – sinology has made an important contribution to our knowledge of Chinese pottery. At that time these texts were taken as a final authority not only for pottery but for the entire field of art. The earthenware objects dug up by the railway builders were found to bear a great resemblance to the aforementioned bronzes. With the encouragement of the texts, this formed the basis not only for the first dating of the ceramic pieces, but for a theory as to their derivation. It was believed that the pottery shapes followed those of the bronzes, that the clay objects were placed in the tombs as substitutes for the fine metal vessels and that they indicated the weaker faith or fortune of the dead they accompanied. Some of the bronze vessels bore inscriptions, which the sinologues were soon able to decipher. They proclaimed that the presence of the vessels in the tomb was intended as a comfort for the prince who had used them on his altar in life.

Another belief of the early days of sinology encouraged by the classic Chinese texts concerned the first appearance of glazed earthenware. It was commonly held that the Chinese first invented, or perhaps copied, the technique of glazing at about the beginning of our era, during the Han dynasty, when rather crude pottery utensils and small figures were covered with a green and brown lead glaze easy to handle in a relatively low burning oven. The experts were convinced that the Chinese knew nothing of aluminous glazes, which contain feldspar and require a very high temperature, before the eleventh century when they first began to produce fine porcelain. Thus, Chinese ceramics were divided in two main groups: the first dug out of tombs (from the earliest times to the end of Sung) called the Early Ceramic Wares, and the second, brought to Europe by the East India Companies and since, made during the Manchu dynasty from c. 1600 to 1900, called the Later Ceramic Wares. Between these two large groups stood the Ming Ceramic Wares, unburied pieces made from about 1400 to 1600.

In the 1920s a Swedish geologist, G. J. Anderson, and later some German commercial airmen found a completely new type of pottery in Honan and Kansu. In form and decoration it revealed the existence of a culture that pre-dated the

V   LARGE PLATE ON THREE SMALL FEET. *35½ cm. diameter. The incised rigid stylisation of the central rosette and the leaves surrounding it are a Persian influence, brought into China by Sassanian refugees, once the rulers of Persia. Driven out by the Arabs, they took refuge in China and brought along their styles in dress, design, music, the dance, colour, and a new way of working silver and gold. However, the mottling, which produces a characteristic liveliness, is a purely Chinese contribution.*   Victoria and Albert Museum, London

period of the bronzes by about a thousand years. It also showed that its makers possessed a technique and feeling for decoration quite remarkable in any civilisation. The majority of these vessels were fairly large, onion shaped, of a brick colour, half hand modelled and half turned on a slow wheel, made of a fine clay and decorated in bold, handsome patterns inspired by foliage and fruit. Very shortly afterwards, a different type of pottery was found in Shantung province, at Lungshan – black, equally finely potted – together with other remains of a pre-bronze culture which indicate that it achieved a level higher than any other on the Eurasian land-mass. It has not been possible to date this ware though it is certain that its beginnings follow the beginnings of the one previously described. Modern Chinese archaeologists believe that Lungshan is the link between the neolithic cultures of China and the great bronze era that suddenly appears in the valley of the Huang Ho where the river makes its huge upward loop, the Shang-Yin culture which produced the first and finest of the bronze vessels we have spoken about. Finally, near Anyang, the site which yielded the bronzes, a fine white pottery has been found incised with patterns similar to those on the bronze vessels. There is, therefore, no doubt that these ceramic utensils were made concurrently with the metal vessels.

How completely these finds upset the existing chronology can well be imagined. Moreover some of the pieces dug up at Anyang were found to bear a hard aluminous glaze which altered the dating for this innovation from the tenth century A.D. to the tenth century B.C.

A re-examination of dates was obviously necessary. One of the systems which has emerged, revolutionary compared to the old, should find favour because it is derived both from a critical perusal of the Chinese texts and from comparisons with the development of other Chinese art forms combined with exact observation of this form in particular. There is no doubt now that in China ceramics had their own organic growth, alongside bronze, stone sculpture, painting and the other art forms. To what extent this new grouping will be accepted it is difficult to say, for scholars are of course, human and *humanum dissidere est*.

In this new scheme all the wares from the neolithic up to and including Han go under the name of Archaic Ceramic Wares. In spite of the fact that most of Han is glazed, and in a technique equal to the succeeding types – that is to say with lead

Plates 8-11, 14   glazes achieved at low temperatures – its style and manner places it in the archaic

VI   JAR. *32 cm. high. The glaze has been applied in an attempt to create a pattern. The generous dimensions and the bold motive, half controlled and half left to nature, are the unusual features of this vessel. Nowhere more than here is the robbery apparent which the porcelain decorators of the seventeenth century perpetrated. They must have dug up one of these vessels and used it to give life to the vast production of 'San Ts'ai', the Three Colours porcelain of the K'ang Hsi period.*   Collection Marchese G. F. Giaquili-Ferrini, Florence

group. It is also excluded from the second group, by reason of its uncompromising name, Classic Ceramic Wares; this covers Chinese pottery from the end of Han down to our own time. The divide coincides with the appearance in China of Buddhism and the great stimulus it provided for all the arts. We know that Indian Buddhism carried resonant echoes of Graeco-Latin influences to China. But even if Classic Ceramic Wares show few affinities with the classicism of Greece and Rome, they answer the general definition of the word 'classic': they are certainly 'of allowed excellence'.

Plates x, 82, 99, 108

It will be useful, before passing on to consider the development of form from archaic to T'ang, to go back to the bronzes and examine them briefly in the light of this new dating. It is not surprising that the early students of Chinese ceramics should have arrived at their conclusions when one considers that the majority of pottery shapes first found were almost direct copies of the Han bronzes excavated nearby. Allowing for evolution and the disappearance of bronze vessels from post-Han tombs it was a logical conclusion that T'ang and the later shapes should have descended from the original bronze prototypes. Other factors contributed to this view. When the T'ang potters invented porcelain they immediately proceeded to use the material to copy the hallowed Han forms of jade objects, which this new material, with its hard, aluminous glaze, so closely resembled. Scholars felt bound to conclude that a passion for the copying of prototypes animated the ceramic producers. And even today we must admit that this was true as regards at least an important section of the potters, although we know that some of their contemporaries were continuously experimenting with daring and successful deviations meant to conform with the technical advances of their craft.

Plate 5

It was only with the discovery of the pre-bronze pottery that it became clear that before bronze vessels started on their own evolution the majority of them had been copies of earthenware shapes. To take a single vessel-form: a baked mud utensil originating from a spindle-shaped container meant to be thrust into the earth so that it should stand upright is assembled in threes to form a tripod with a

VII *THREE ENTERTAINERS. 25 cm. high. The central figure is a dancer getting ready for her performance, while the other two are, of course, musicians. The three represent a type of foreigner, from Kuchā in Eastern Turkestan, who gained immediate approval from the early T'ang Chinese for their grace and accomplishments in spite of their 'barbarian' origin. They came into China together with Persians in the guise of entertainers. Along with their charm, they brought a mode of dress which was presently adopted even though it differed radically from the flowing robes the Chinese had always worn. The long sleeve, even if in time it lost some of its narrowness, remained a Chinese fashion till recently. Like the foot, the naked hand was considered a thing of intimacy, and its occasional revelation among the folds of the sleeve has been a womanly exercise celebrated in poetry, drama and the dance. Until lately this delicate ware was placed in the Sui period. Now it is dated early T'ang.*

Collection H. E. Baron Jo van der Elst, Brussels

common mouth, suitable for cooking food over a fire. This figure in its transubstantiation joins the company of the ritualistic bronze vessels under the name of *li*, soon to be modified into the *ting*, the *ho*, the *chüeh* and the *hsien*. How important these creations have been to Chinese culture can be seen from the fact that the greatness of Shang is reflected in the power, the decoration and splendid execution of the hallowed bronzes and from the ritualistic importance of these metal vessels in the fantastic (though perfectly ordered) world of that epoch.

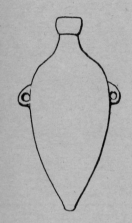

Left: the clay prototypes
of the bronze *li*

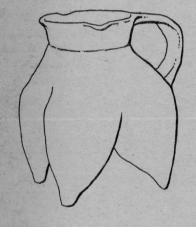

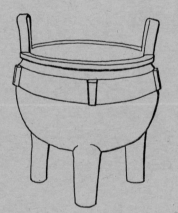

Right: the bronze
vessels *ting* and *ho*

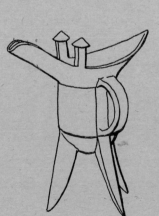

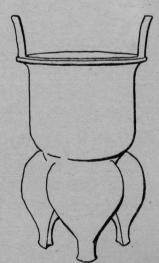

Right: the bronze vessels
chüeh and *hsien*

THE TRANSFORMATION of the ceramic shapes from archaic to classic extended over a period of four centuries, between the end of Han and the beginning of T'ang. The change is one of form and, through this, of feeling. At last the marriage of function and beauty, begun in the late Chou period, has been consummated. For it is in the change of feeling – in the change of form – much more than in any consideration of altered materials, glazes and techniques that one epoch ends and another begins.

These four centuries are important in the evolution of China's history. In them Buddhism begins and fulfils its proselytising mission bringing to China a vital infusion of new artistic points of view that first shakes, is then absorbed by and finally provides an effective stimulus to China's own artistic genius. For a better understanding of this impact which, as we shall see, occurs in the glory of T'ang, it will be useful if we examine, if only briefly, the artistic production of the potter during these four hundred years of transition.

The expectation that the production of the T'ang potter might simply be a continuation of the green and brown glazed pottery of the Han dynasty is belied by an innovation which finds its way into the tombs of the later years of that period. Utensils of a stone-hard, resonant substance are dug up that only differ from porcelain in not being white and translucent, though the body is covered by a glaze totally different from that of pottery, as it is aluminous, truly feldspathic. First found and studied by an American, Berthold Laufer, this grey-bodied ware is given the name of 'proto-porcelain'. The forms are executed with great verve and decorated with graffito designs, often done with a comb, over which the olive-brown glaze is poured with striking effect. As in the lead-glazed pottery of the earlier Han, some figures and animals in this ware too have been found, doubtless intended as tomb decoration.

The importance of this discovery becomes clear when we realize that this is the first appearance of 'porcelain', even if not in its complete form, for whose manufacture a far greater knowledge and technical skill are required than for pottery, however gaudily glazed. Suffice it to say that in Europe a first attempt made under the Medici was abandoned, and it was not until 1710 that a German, Johann Friedrich Boettger, succeeded at last in building an oven capable of creating and maintaining the high temperatures required for the fusion of porcelain-clays. Apart from its historical importance, this ware has a bearing on this study in that it is in T'ang that it finally achieves its complete nobility, for in T'ang the white-burning *kaolin* is first added to ever more refined feldspathic clays to achieve at last an element which is hard, impermeable even when unglazed, ringing, white and translucent – in other words, the true porcelain that appears with *Shing Yao*.

In earthenware, probably because of gaps in archaeological knowledge, there is very little real evidence to link the green and brown glazed funerary ware of the Han dynasty with that of T'ang. It is at the beginning of Han – about 200 B.C. –

Plates 2, 4-8, 11 that there suddenly appears the religious fashion of burying clay models of houses, furniture, farms, animals and servants together with the vessels containing food and drink for the deceased. Leaving till later a description of the religious principles that governed these practices, let us examine this tomb furniture a little more closely, for this makes it easier to understand the strides made by the potter between Han and T'ang. The vessels, as crude as all the manufacture of this and the previous periods, consist of certain types which are repeated again and again

Plate 14 with only the slightest variations: a strange drum-shaped receptacle resting on three feet and covered by a mountain-shaped lid; a cylindrical jar similar to the

Plates 3, 5 bronze shape known as *lien*; and a number of wine and grain jars copied, too, from bronze shapes, simple and vigorous, often shrewdly modified to conform with the exigencies of clay, at other times as shrewdly adapted to make full use of the freedom which that material allows. Other shapes are culled from the vast bronze repertory, and many of them are, together with the more common ones, precursors of those we shall meet in T'ang. One wine vessel in particular heralds the roundness – the classicism – of the T'ang forms: a large-bellied jar decorated with a deep band in which mounted horsemen in moulded bas-relief chase lions and other animals in a surprisingly naturalistic manner much closer in feeling to the

Plate 10 Near East than to anything in China, if one excludes the small animistic bronzes found in the Ordos desert.

VIII MILITARY ATTENDANT. *22 cm. high. The simplicity and the felicity of the gold and blue combination is enhanced by the unglazed face and hands. The head-dress in the shape of a bird with folded wings found on warriors, of which the one worn by the mounted man on Plate XI is an elaboration, and the attitude of the hands on both, lead one to suspect that they are effigies of uniformed standard bearers. While the facial characteristics are not clear enough to allow us to be exact about the type, the garb is distinctly Persian. The starched lapels turned back are one version of the Persian tunic which when closed becomes round at the neck.*   *Seattle Art Museum*

The salient characteristic of all these Han forms is that they have suddenly acquired a freedom and power quite absent in preceding wares. Their early appearance, very early in relation to actual Buddhist penetration, does make one ponder on the accepted assumptions regarding the influence of Buddhism on the evolution that finally results in T'ang. These changed shapes, so much freer from the traditional tenets that had fettered the earlier craftsmen, make one wonder whether the swing from archaic to classical did not in fact begin before the Buddhist influence was felt, especially if we share the suspicion of some modern Chinese students that the proto-porcelain wares, so wide in scope and breathing so much freedom, began even before Han.

However that may be, with the beginning of our era there begins a development in pottery that results in ever greater freedom, especially in the creation of tomb figures, which, from being rigid and even clumsy, become, through the Six Dynasties (265-598) increasingly realistic. To the Six Dynasties is ascribed a pottery, grey-black in its unglazed body, decorated with unfired pigments over a white slip. The models found represent warriors mounting richly caparisoned horses oddly similar to the jousting steeds of our Middle Ages; Bactrian camels sensitively executed, often resting and laden down with the wares they have carried from the Far West; and female figures of a striking and effective simplicity which,

Plates 16, 19, 20, 24   more than any of the other examples, constitute a link between Han and what is to come. Here Buddhist influence is already strong. A comparison between these earthenware sculptures and those hewn by Buddhists in the stone caves during the Northern Wei period of the Six Dynasties helps us not only to date these figures but also to identify their religious significance. In the female forms the calm attitude and serene simplicity certainly imply a Buddhist prompting.

Another ware must here be mentioned not only for its revolutionary technical features, but also for the obvious influence it exerted on T'ang pottery. *Yüeh yao*,

Plates 12, 13, 17   generally attributed to the third, fourth and fifth centuries of our era, is an obvious relation of Laufer's proto-porcelain, referred to on an earlier page, which more modern scholars believe begins as early as the sixth century B.C. Found in Shensi, Kiangsu, Korea and Fukien, it has a very hard grey body containing *kaolin*. First covered with a slip, the body has an olive brown glaze poured over it which more often than not stops short of the foot. While some forms are strongly

IX   *Lady attendant with scarf. 27 cm. high. The unglazed head has been painted with unfired pigments which reveal the great taste for maquillage that prevailed during T'ang and in time, under influence from Turkey and Persia, became an aberration justly condemned by the T'ang poets. A pleasantly lifelike effect comes from the perfunctory application of the pigments. It may be that this is a symptom of mass-production problems, though the costly blue glaze does not seem to bear it out. The scarf covering the shoulders, but often worn over the head, is a fashion which started in the early T'ang period, with the first advent of Persian travellers to China.   Collection Dott. Alberto Giuganino, Rome*

reminiscent of the late Chou bronze animals, others herald T'ang – unless indeed, they are made during T'ang, through which period they probably continued, linking up eventually with the Lung Chuan celadons of the Sung dynasty.

Plates XIX, 15, 21-23, 25, 105, 117, 118

Plate 15

Shing Yao is at last the pure porcelain, produced in the T'ang dynasty. It fulfils the exacting demands of Western experts, by ringing when struck and being transparent and white. Used only rarely for sculpture (a striking lion biting its hind paw in the Victoria and Albert Museum in London is the only example that comes to mind) this ware was the medium used by the T'ang potter for the finest precursors of the porcellaneous stoneware of the Sung – vessels, cosmetic boxes,

Plate 23

bowls and certain oddly shaped receptacles which museums are beginning to classify as spittoons.

These two wares are of the greatest importance in themselves as technical achievements, and also because they announce the new force that was to produce such marvels in the years to come.

To the succeeding Sui dynasty (581-618) is attributed a very attractive group

Plate VII

of figurines of pinkish-white pottery glazed over in cream and sometimes decorated with blue and red pigments. But, like the black-grey ladies described who are

Plates 2, 4

now more and more often attributed to Han, these are straining more in the T'ang direction. It is increasingly felt that the effort to fill the gap between Han and T'ang has encouraged attributions which are not sufficiently corroborated by archaeological facts.

Whether or not this hiatus between the two great dynasties will ever be filled, as far as ceramics is concerned, we are in no doubt that with the beginning of the seventh century the moment of Buddhist saturation, of the consummation of the marriage between Buddhism and China's artistic genius, has arrived. It is here that the so-called Classic Ceramic Ware of China begins. The magnificence of this period in China's history will become apparent when we investigate the meaning of the wares that these people insisted on burying with their dead. At this point it will be useful to pass to some considerations regarding the development of form in utensils.

*   *   *

X VASE IN THE FORM OF A BOTTLE. *24 cm. high. The dramatic abstraction achieved by the poured glazes, so Chinese in conception, makes one forget that underneath it is a Roman shape that began its pilgrimage in Roman Alexandria, is then found in the hands of the first Graeco-Buddhist images of Afghanistan and Northern Persia, was carried to Ghandara in Northern India and from there, through Gupta and the Wei caverns of China – always resting in the left hand of the Buddha – to the potter's wheel of T'ang times. Once there, this form achieved that 'organic' aspect which is the hall-mark of all T'ang shapes.* British Museum, London

It is difficult to escape the belief that every Chinese potter was basically striving to evolve his utensil's shape in a manner which can only be described as organic, in the sense that the evolution of nature's utensil-shapes is described as organic. Surely no other people has so endeavoured to emulate nature as the Chinese or brought this principle to such high perfection.

What are the factors that determine form in the creation of a utensil? One is, of course, that human element which we have tried to describe earlier: the urge towards self-expression, or the artistic will. This we will classify as the first factor, because were not the artistic will more important than the other factors in the production of any utensil, then utensils would be alike everywhere; and because if we identify the particular artistic will of the Chinese with the 'organic intent' we have just spoken of we will readily see how amply it overcomes the next two factors which are: the nature of the material the craftsman works with and the use for which the vessel is intended. The need to balance these three factors – and having done so to maintain that balance – engendered a very slow evolution in the form of vessels, hampered yet further by the rigorous control of apprentices who were strongly discouraged from indulging their inventive caprices.

Art historians maintain that only a violent clash with a superior culture can hasten such a slow process, even though they admit that the invention of new techniques may have the same effect. They believe that such a clash occurred in China with the advent of Buddhism from India; and though the Chinese genius for fusing the form, technique and functionality of a vessel won over the years, there is no doubt that a vessel made two hundred years before T'ang is less akin to one made in T'ang than it is to one made fifteen centuries earlier.

When we examine the forms of these early pots, however, we must consider that the Chinese, a nation more devoted to tradition than any other, included in their 'artistic will' a very strong attachment to memories. Early on, certain clay forms were established which were far removed from the obvious shape given by a potter's wheel. Clay objects so abound in the remains of any early culture that it almost looks as though clay pots were the only utensils our ancestors ever used. The truth is that in China, before clay, utensils were made of wood, bamboo, gourd,

XI HORSE WITH RIDER. *43 cm. high. The face and head-dress, unglazed, are painted with unfired pigments. Here, too, the garment is Persian, but not much is yet known about the unusual hat which seems inspired like that on plate VIII by a bird about to spread its wings. A hole through the fists indicates that the figure was made to carry a standard which, made probably of wood or lacquer, has since disintegrated. Many of the tomb figures bore additions and embellishments in other materials. Horses have been found with a runnel down the length of the upper neck, and a hole at the end of the spine. These cavities were surely meant to take real horsehair manes and tails, as some later porcelain figures are adorned with wisps of real human hair threaded through holes under the nose and chin.*

Collection Dott. Alberto Giuganino, Rome

leather, all now perished, but the shapes of which are found again and again in the gamut of ceramic forms right down to our day. Having been accepted in the tradition, in what is best described as the 'aesthetic complex' of the potter, they were never abandoned. It is difficult to say where, in the uneventful evolution before the advent of Buddhism, the 'aesthetic complex' of the potter became the 'non-inventive self-consciousness' handed down from master potter to apprentice. Yet in considering the development of China's artistic works, it is important that both attitudes be borne in mind. The Chinese character has always been perhaps of all people's the most devoted to formalism and tradition, the most loath to tamper with first principles. To this awed respect for the past which has become an artistic creed, a whole pantheon of forms is dedicated. Soon we find the forms migrating from one material to the other; and very early this transubstantiation of hallowed forms becomes an aesthetic principle. As early as the fifteenth century B.C. pottery shapes, as we have already seen, become bronze forms, to revert to their original clay state ten centuries later. If this clay-bronze-clay journey is more obvious than the other ones, it is only because the ductility of clay and of fused metal facilitate the shift. Wood, silver, lacquer, stone make their own demands which discourage this interplay. Yet the Chinese choice of a ductile substance for his most complete three-dimensional self-expression may well have another reason – a subtle knowledge that clay, made infinitely more plastic by the spinning potter's wheel, allows a direct communion between the artist and his creation, that it permits the artist to reveal himself by only the slightest pressure of his wet hands on the spinning clay.

* * *

Nothing better reveals the Chinese potter's desire to imitate nature than the stanza from a Chinese poem: 'Let neither man nor animal wandering through the forest recognise the potter's work therein arranged.'

What is the philosophy that leads to this desire? It is a view of life, a religion, so different from our own that it is impossible to describe in this space, involving as it does all the other expressions of Chinese art, the mass of Chinese poetry, of

XII LARGE BACTRIAN CAMEL. *76 cm. high. The saddle-cloth, this piece's most unusual feature, has been applied over the glaze in unfired pigments. It bears a vigorous decoration in blue and red reminiscent of the frescoes in the temples of Pi Yuen Ssu, near Peking, and in the T'ang tombs recently uncovered in Loyang and published by the Government of the Chinese People's Republic. The gold band around the saddle-cloth is a rare feature on glazed pottery. It is justified here by the presence of the unfired pigments which, over unglazed pieces, are often accompanied by decorations in gold. The treatment of the head, composed of bold geometric planes, is in sympathy with twentieth-century art. Another unusual feature of this splendid beast is the subtle moss-green colouring of one of the glazes. See detail in plate.*

Collection Avv. Umberto Ortolani, Rome

Confucianism, Taoism and Buddhism — and perhaps underlying all this, the harsh country in which this people lives, tamed by nature's cruel excesses. Here all philosophies become religions. To the Chinese exorcism is merely a means of survival in the face of violent reality.

Nature is awe-inspiring and frightening. But it also instructs. It is incomprehensible but it is also the ultimate perfection. In design, for instance, the Chinese observed that nature abhors the broken line. So, the tight contour of the apple became the ideal, along with the firm design of the cherry, the perfect roundnesses that occur again and again in the natural world. The Unbroken Line became the Chinese aesthetic dream. Nothing reveals this better than a comparison between a Greek vase and a Chinese jar. While in the first the authorship of man stands revealed, in the second the maker has been obliterated by his striving to synthesise a natural object.

Plates XVI, XXVI, XXXII, 100, 118

It did not happen all at once. The miracle lies as much in its development as in its existence. Through the ages we see all manner of changes discarded or mutations maintained. Above all forms that begin as square, like the bronze *hu* of the Han period, end, after acquiring ever more sides, as fluted rotundities in the Sung dynasty. The spindly knife-legs on the bronze *chüeh* become harmonious feet discreetly protruding under the vessel's belly like those of a pug. The tripod is a favourite with the Chinese potter, followed by another vessel originally based on a high, hollow upturned box which first becomes hexagonal, then round and finally smaller and smaller until it forms a harmonious whole with the higher portion. As with the tripod, it would seem as though a reconciliation of the vessel with the earth from which it has sprung were slowly accomplished.

Plate IV

Plates 1, 103, 111, 115,

In spite of the innumerable variations to please this or that current taste, the general trend is so strongly marked that very soon the student can count on it as a workable basis for chronology, no small boon in a sphere where the reports of historians have always been more romantic than trustworthy. It is through a study of this *Wanderung* of form more than through any other exercise that at last the dividing line between the Archaic and the Classic becomes clear. To illustrate this in a homely way let us say that its completion is at hand when the farmer (archaic forms) becomes the city dweller (classic forms). This moment is in T'ang.

XIII OFFERING DISH RESTING ON THREE FEET. *29 cm. diameter. The uninteresting flatness of a plate, even when it rests on three short feet — a descendant of the bronze p'an — invites a decoration that will not detract from or interfere with the utensil's shape. The lotus bud, blossom and leaf has been borrowed from nature to be turned into a pattern that ripples at the edges and turns like a wheel. The underside and the feet of the dish are almost entirely covered by a gold-coloured glaze which succeeds perfectly in giving greater value to the sapphire blue of the rim. The general attempt of these pieces to imitate the costly silver and gold plate of the Persians is particularly obvious in this one.*

Collection Marchese G. Litta-Modignani, Capalbio

Whenever the Chinese dream of imitating nature, of achieving the Unbroken Line, may have begun, it is certain that it is at last fulfilled in the art of the T'ang potter.

XIV LADY AT HER TOILETTE. *26 cm. high. The fine modelling, the unusual posture, the rich glaze comprising the entire palette of the T'ang potter-sculptor, indicate that this statuette must have been made to accompany a rather exalted personage into the other world. Reports on the great vogue for make-up by T'ang historians coincide with reports of woman's importance in that period. But, while the mundane means to achieve this were never neglected, T'ang women also wrote memorable poems, painted important pictures and became, too deeply even, involved in affairs of state (see page 134). The position that the leg has assumed here is one dear to Chinese women, as is the abandoned, empty shoe, for in their land the unshod foot has always been an instrument of coquetry. The lady is seated on a sort of drum with a narrow waist and with straps criss-crossing it in a way to suggest leather. Perhaps this piece of furniture again shows the influence the nomadic people of Central Asia exerted on the Chinese in the T'ang period.* Collection Signorina Paola Varzi, Galliate

Notes on Plates 1-25
(The precursors of T'ang)

1 THREE-FOOTED VESSEL. 10½ cm. high. Dark grey pottery with hatching. Perhaps an earthenware ancestor of the bronze *ting*. Archaic. *Barling of Mount Street, Ltd., London.*

2 FIGURE OF A DANCER. 41 cm. high. Unglazed grey pottery with traces of white, black and buff pigments. *Collection Mrs M. Verney, London.*

3 VASE. 58 cm. high. Unglazed grey pottery with traces of a design in white, ochre and red pigments. Han dynasty. *Collection Oswald T. Falk, Esq., Oxford.*

4 FEMALE FIGURE. 38 cm. high. Unglazed grey pottery with slight traces of pigment. Han dynasty. *Collection Oswald T. Falk, Esq., Oxford.*

5 VASE. 49 cm. high. Unglazed grey pottery with a design in buff pigment. An earthenware replica of the bronze *hu* of Han times. Han dynasty. *Collection Dr Ernst Hauswedell, Hamburg.*

6 HORSE. 35½ cm. long. Unglazed grey pottery with slight traces of pigments. Han dynasty. *Collection Dr Umberto Ortolani, Rome.*

7 KNEELING FIGURE. 31¼ cm. high. Unglazed grey pottery with traces of white slip. Perhaps an actor (see plate 28). Han dynasty. *Barling of Mount Street, Ltd., London.*

8 GROUP OF FIGURES PLAYING A GAME. Standing figure, 25 cm. high. Green thick glaze turned iridescent in parts, over a red earthenware body. Han dynasty. *British Museum, London.*

9 ROUND BOX. 17½ cm. diameter. Brown glaze over a red earthenware body. Han dynasty. *Barling of Mount Street, Ltd., London.*

10 JAR. 56 cm. high. Green glaze over a red earthenware body. Han dynasty. *Collection R. Penrose Hocker, Esq., London.*

11 PAIR OF OIL LAMPS. 28 cm. high. Thick green glaze turned iridescent, over a red earthenware body. *Collection Marchese G. F. Giaquili-Ferrini, Florence.*

12 HORSE. 36¼ cm. high. Olive-green glaze over a hard porcellaneous body. *Yüeh Yao.* Third to fifth centuries. *Collection J. B. Nowell, Esq., London.*

13 EWER. 22 cm. high. Olive-green glaze over a buff coloured 'proto-porcelain'. *Yüeh Yao.* This ware, generally ascribed to the third to fifth centuries of our era, is now believed to have begun, even if in a slightly different and coarser paste, in the seventh century B.C. The elegance of this form would indicate that it went on being manufactured well after the fifth century, surely through T'ang if not through the Five Dynasties. *Collection Professor Roberto Ago, Rome.*

14 'HILL' JAR. 29 cm. high. Thick green glaze turned iridescent in part, over a red earthenware body. Han dynasty. *Collection Marchese G. F. Giaquili-Ferrini, Florence.*

15 LION SCRATCHING HIS EAR. 14 cm. high. *Shing-Yao* porcelain. Modelled pieces are very rare in this early porcelain, and this one is among the few that are known. Under the Sung dynasty the potters of *Ying Ching (Ch'ing Pai)* ware took to modelling in porcelain. *Victoria and Albert Museum, London.*

16 BALL PLAYER. 10½ cm. high. Unglazed dark grey pottery with traces of pigment. Wei dynasty. *Collection Oswald T. Falk, Esq., Oxford.*

17 FANTASTIC ANIMAL. 14 cm. long. Olive-brown glaze over a hard porcellaneous body. *Yüeh Yao.* Third to fifth centuries. *Collection Marchese G. F. Giaquili-Ferrini, Florence.*

18 DETAIL OF COLOUR PLATE XII showing the saddle-cloth applied in unfired pigments over the glaze and decorated with blue and red scrolls.

19 PAIR OF WARRIORS. 27 cm. high. Dark grey pottery with traces of white slip and black and red pigments. Late Wei dynasty. *Barling of Mount Street, Ltd., London.*

20 CAMEL WITH CAMELEER. 18 cm. high. Unglazed grey pottery with traces of white slip. Wei dynasty. *Collection Sir Alan Barlow, Wendover.*

21 STEM CUP. 8½ cm. high. *Shing Yao.* White glaze over egg-shell-thin porcelain. Glass stem cups of this shape from the Roman world were found in Korea, and this may well be a copy done in the new miraculous element, as near to glass as to pottery. *Royal Ontario Museum, Toronto.*

22 COSMETIC BOX. 11½ cm. high. *Shing Yao* porcelain with white glaze. The two nipples, so decorative on the unencumbered surfaces, are meant to show the proper fit of the two parts. *Royal Ontario Museum, Toronto.*

23 LOW VASE (perhaps a spittoon). 10 cm. high. *Shing Yao* porcelain with a cream coloured glaze. *Royal Ontario Museum, Toronto.*

24 PAIR OF PRIESTS. 51 cm. high. Unglazed grey pottery with traces of white slip. Wei dynasty. *T. Y. King, Jr., Hongkong.*

25 EWER. 31¼ cm. high. *Shing Yao* porcelain. Cream glaze. This shape is derived from a Persian leather bottle. The leaf decoration at the bottom of the ornamental seam is Hellenistic. *Royal Ontario Museum, Toronto.*

2

8

9

10

14

15

16

17

21

22

23

24

THE T'ANG ERA, which Sir Alan Barlow has described as one of the most cultured periods the world has yet seen, began in the field of art and learning as a reaction against the exaggerations of the age before. The last emperor of the preceding dynasty, Yang Ti, deserves more than passing reference, not only because the Sui dynasty founded by his father is the herald of T'ang after four hundred years of dismemberment and near anarchy, but also because Yang Ti was certainly one of the greatest patrons of the arts history has yet recorded. Chinese literary gentlemen of the succeeding eras looked back on this monarch with wistfulness and great affection. They describe his life as entirely devoted to the beautifying of Loyang and his empire; he loved to travel by water and these journeys had the enchantment of a continuous fairy feast. Less celebrated is his downfall, brought about by a revolt of his people who had been bled white by corvées and taxation to pay for his aesthetic excesses and the giant constructions of canals which he undertook more, some suspect, for his pleasure than for national expediency. The revolt which broke out and led to his assassination was precipitated by a disastrous campaign to subjugate Korea. It led to the advent of T'ang.

It was an era of great and original men living in a world of ferment, excitement and change. Buddhism had been pouring tracts, art and originality more and more overtly into a disorganised China by three main means and routes – the merchants on the Silk Road, the warriors on the Steppes and the holy men across the sea. Beginning by conditioning those barbaric tribes which had conquered northern China and had no Confucian or other state philosophy to be overcome, they attacked the Chinese more directly, even if insidiously at first, by disguising themselves under the phraseology of Taoism, an elephantine *tour de force* if one considers that Lao Tzu had preached a doctrine of finality the very opposite to that of Buddha.

There was, to be sure, reaction in both areas: violent repression at the hands

The opulent age.
Sacrifice and substitute

57

of northern rulers who were very rapidly succumbing to Chinese tradition, and intense theological casuistry by Taoist monks who went so far as to proclaim Buddha one of the Taoist Immortals, the one in fact who had been sent to India to teach a Taoism simple enough for barbarians. This sophistry, this overflow from one religious vessel into another, this race for favour at court, was to continue throughout the centuries in China. Yet by the year 471 A.D. Buddhist success in the North was so complete that some of the greatest sculptures the world has seen, all Buddhist, adorned the caves of Yung Kang and were safe under royal patronage. By 525 Bodhidarma, a famous Indian Buddhist monk, was in Nanking preaching the Ch'an doctrine and Chinese pilgrims had been travelling to Indian Buddhist monasteries for the past hundred years. In 570 another great man of those turbulent years, Wen Kung, king of the Wei, fired by Buddhist devotion and a desire for self-effacement, gathered all the beggars of Loyang in his private park and, donning mendicant's garb, went forth to beg for them, accompanied by his court ladies likewise disguised.

It is from Yung Kang and the Lung Men caves situated near the new Wei capital of Loyang that the Chinese craze for sculpture originated. The Indian missionaries, in order to render their work easier, turned their backs on the iconoclasm of their previous experience. They found the most effective prototype of the man-god in what Greek and Roman sculptors had left behind in India. Bringing this art first to what is now modern Afghanistan and Iran with great success, the proselytisers carried it thenceforth wherever they went, allowing local taste to modify, radically alter or even, if necessary, substitute indigenous forms for the prototypes. In Afghanistan the Aryan faces assume an expression that

XV   HEAD REST. *19 cm. long. Such pillows are rarer in the T'ang dynasty than in Sung, and the treatment of the infant is nearer that of the Tzuchow potter who was active in the latter period. But the earthenware body, the nature more than the colours of the glazes, the 'roundness' of the object, place it more securely in T'ang. The idea of the piece is gentle enough to fit into any Chinese age, for the Chinese have always made a cult of babies. It is just this conflict between style and material, between colouring and glazes pushing the piece in two opposite directions which makes it one of the most unusual here illustrated.*
Collection Marchese G. Litta-Modignani, Capalbio

XVI   JAR. *24 cm. high. The honey colour on this vessel is unusually fine — but it is often accompanied by flakings such as are visible here, so it seems that procuring such a rich colour must have jeopardised the success of the firing. Such blemishes are easily — and often — restored, as are the chips at the mouth of this jar. But some collectors prefer to leave their pieces in the state in which they were found, and must often, indeed, patiently undo the work of restorers in order to bring their acquisitions to their 'first' state. It can be asserted that the one shown here is the most typical of T'ang shapes — either because it was the most apt to emit the effluvia of which the spirits must sup or because it fulfilled most completely the Chinese dream of organic form.*
Collection H. E. Giovanni Gronchi, Rome

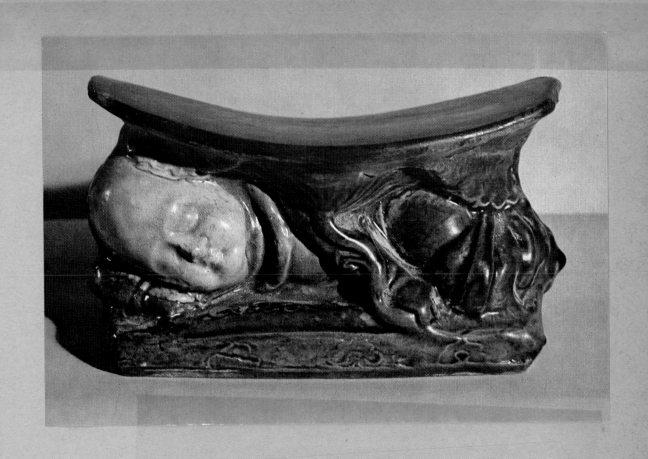

reveals the purity of the doctrine as it made its first impact abroad; in India itself the Gupta transformation speaks of a sensuality long present in Hinduism; and in China, in the caverns of Yung Kang and Lung Men, the flowing Graeco-Roman draperies take on an angularity that tries to merge the human form of the new gods into a geometry reflecting the Chinese conception of the universe. In time the angularity vanishes, the mounting flood of Indian evangelism compels a rotundity, a greater naturalism. But the human forms maintain an otherworldliness even within the confines of the hieratic rules, a concern with the supernatural that scorns the flesh and gives the enormous figures an appearance of levitation.

With the beginning of T'ang, Buddhist penetration is complete and the roundness, the opulence, the relatively large size of some of the tomb furnishings reflect the style prevailing in sculpture, for example in the giant stone figures which we encounter hewn into the rock of Lung Men during this period. One Buddha, sitting in the posture of meditation, resplendent in his clinging draperies and placed in front of a flaming nimbus, is forty-five feet in height. The numerous bodhisattvas of Tien Lung Shan are bejewelled and sensuously draped beauties ambiguous as to sex. Chinese sculpture has come as near as it will ever come to its Indian model. Naturalism and freedom of conception pervade every artistic manifestation. This is China's moment of greatness, artistic, political, military and cultural. T'ai Tsung the Great, the most important monarch to sit on the Celestial Throne, had conquered the empire for his father. By force of arms, during the twenty-two years of his reign (627-649) he extended China's boundaries as far north as Turfan, as far west as Kashgar and as far south as Yarkand. In administration and statemanship, he undertook and completed the re-establishment of Chinese unity which had been left incomplete by the Sui. He unified and gave new force to the Confucian canons, the all-important ethical system on which Chinese Government had rested since the Han, by imposing a uniform reading of the texts. Later, in their new arrangement, they were carved on stone as an enduring code of law. This strict reversion to Confucianism by an early T'ang emperor cannot be considered solely as a reaction against Buddhist laxity, for the instinct of traditionalism is never long absent in Chinese affairs. Nor can the war on Buddhism have been nearly as severe as it was to be at the end of T'ang itself for we find, in spite of an imperial edict limiting the number of Buddhist temples, an early T'ang inscription on a statue now in a Japanese collection to the effect that

XVII DEEP BOWL. *18 cm. diameter. Here the Sassanian influence is again apparent in the incised decoration, so similar to the repoussé patterns found on Persian silver of the period. But the stained-glass mood given to the piece by the quiet background glazes is a purely Chinese achievement. The faults that can be seen inside are unlikely to be spur marks. These humps of paste are too irregular for that, and are more probably caused by impurities in the glaze, bursting in the firing, which may be responsible for the flaking rim as well.*

Victoria and Albert Museum, London

this forceful effigy of Buddha was commissioned by one Ma Chou, one of the emperor T'ai Tsung's own ministers. Even before the end of this emperor's reign we witness the re-emergence of Buddhism with the triumphant return of Chinese pilgrims – who did not, indeed, need to travel far to imbibe the creed. By 630 all the routes into China – the whole of the Silk Road, Siberia, Java and Sumatra – had become ardently Buddhist. An impenetrable belt had been created around China and the emperor himself at last welcomed back the most important of the pilgrims, the immortal Hsüan Tsang. Buddhism had come to the moment of its greatest splendour. The emperor's successors, especially the widowed empress Wu, actually supported rather than merely tolerated the religious and missionary zeal of the Buddhists. In accordance with this triumph, the vast number of Buddhist effigies of this period bear an expression which is powerful rather than graceful, and self-assured rather than tender.

The court, in its imperial maturity, had become the gravitational point of all manner of splendours. At Ch'ang-An, the capital, constellations of painters, poets, artists of genius revolved around the imperial orb. The 'dolce stil nuovo' in poetry, begun one hundred years earlier, here came to full bloom. The emperor Ming Huang (712-756) was himself an outstanding poet, and his favourite concubine, the notorious Yang Kuei Fei, vied with him in distributing emoluments to the literati and artists of the court. A predilection for talent broke down the strict barriers of rank. Li Po, king of poets, though half a foreigner, was a favourite in spite of his quaint ways and his addiction to wine. His poem Swallow in Flight, a paean to Yang Kuei Fei's beauty of form and spirit, remains a monument more imperishable than historic truth itself. Chinese lore would have this much beloved genius end his days by trying to embrace the moon's reflection in the water, when drunk one night, and drowning – as it would have another beloved contemporary of Li Po, the painter Wu Tao Tzu, disappear from this world by walking out of it through one of his own painted landscapes. At this enlightened court were other men of fame, artists who carried on the tradition of painters such as Yen Li Pen who, under the widowed empress Wu, had held a very important post in the government. Before the concubine Yang Kuei Fei succumbed to her passion for one of her grooms, the imperial côterie had included Tu Fu, China's greatest poet. His verse succeeds in giving a measure of the spiritual atmosphere of that remarkable time. The two great painters Han Kan and Chang Hsüan were also guests in

XVIII OGRE. *70 cm. high. This fear-inspiring animal, reminiscent of the Egyptian sphinx, is a descendant of the Shang-Yin goddess of the earth Shê, now become a tomb guardian against evil spirits and morbid influences. Its ugliness and fierceness is in line with the 'psychological warfare' with which the living defended their dead against the evil spirits of the nether world. Considered aesthetically, it belongs to the Chinese scheme whereby beauty will shine the more when set off by ungainliness.* Collection T. Y. King, Jr, Hongkong

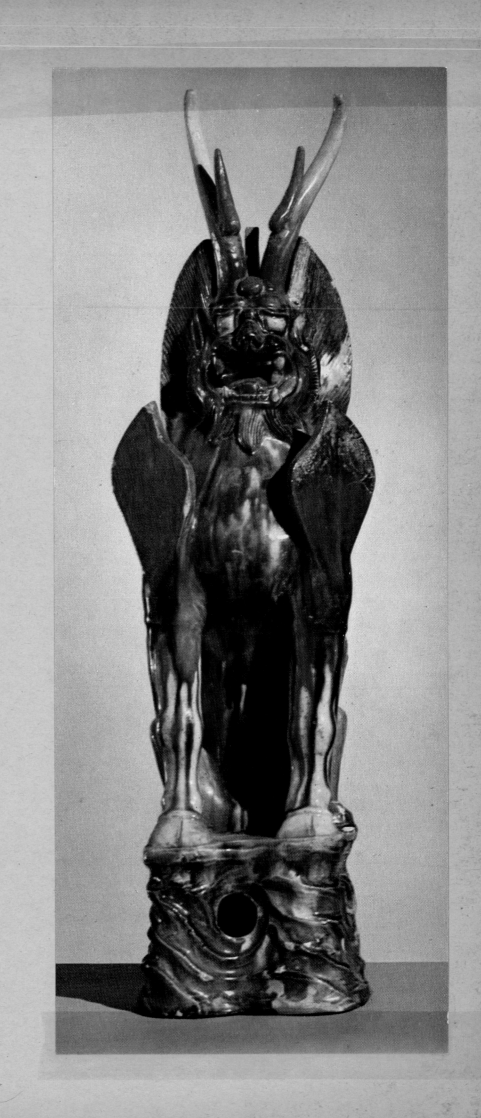

Ming Huang's palace. The one a painter of horses and the other a painter of women, they gave the greatest pleasure to the emperor who delighted in both subjects. Only copies and copies of copies have come down to us but they suffice to confirm the genius of their work. Indeed the very earthenware horses and ladies found in the tombs of the period and made by mere artisans strike us as important works of art. For be it remarked here that not only earthenware but sculpture itself, the great sculpture of Wei, Sui and T'ang, has always been regarded by the Chinese as a craft, the rank of artist being granted only to the painter-scholar.

After the first shock of the palace revolt instigated by Yang Kuei Fei and executed by her menial lover, and a second uprising even bloodier than the first, the Confucian councillors of the court did not hesitate once again to blame Buddhism for the disasters. In 845 an imperial edict ordered a wholesale massacre of Buddhists and a systematic destruction of their temples. Though the last T'ang emperors revoked the edict and provided the Buddhists with a nimbus of martyrdom, the fall of T'ang has remained in the mind of many as the sign of a divine Buddhist will. In 906 the imperial armies were overcome by the mutinous garrisons of the extreme south, and the glorious reign was over, followed by an anarchic state of affairs no better than that which had preceded the glorious Sui-T'ang epoch, even though it only lasted a little over fifty years.

* * *

In the course of these three hundred years of T'ang splendour, and more particularly in its first hundred years as we shall see, a fashion broke out which we, detached as we are from our departed and with our horror of death, may well consider fantastic. It became the mode to use the age-old custom of tomb-furnishing for purposes of social competition. The mechanics of this practice are revealed to us by a chronicler of the times, who tells us that the dead were accompanied to their grave by great throngs and that along the procession's route, in pavilions and tents, the mourners were entertained with food, wine, actors, acrobats, circuses and women. In these temporary structures the furniture which was to adorn the tomb was on view. Of all that panoply of pleasure the earthenware tomb furniture is all that has remained. But the quantities found are enough to

XIX EWER. *20 cm. high. The fusion of functionalism and form achieved here seems to be as nearly complete as is possible to human hands. Perhaps more than any other piece shown it reveals the Chinese potter's preoccupation with procuring a synthesis of the forms in nature. This ware, called Shing Yao by the Chinese, is already porcelain — made seven centuries before it was successfully attempted in Europe. The opulence of T'ang is unaltered in the harder element, though a new austerity shines from the harder glaze. Present in this form is the elegance of Sung and of the vast ceramic production that is soon to come. The dynasty after T'ang, the Ming, will react by emulating the power of the T'ang forms so lovingly that they transform them into baroque.*
Collection Ing. Piero Rossi, Rome

64

reveal how widespread was the custom and how it permeated society from the highest to the lowest. They reveal, too, that a chronicle's account of the financial disasters of some families in their effort to keep up with their neighbours is more than probable. Before the first hundred years of the T'ang dynasty had run out, an imperial edict was promulgated laying down strict specifications for the practice of tomb decoration. It was decreed that a personage above the fourth rank could be accompanied by no more than 40 pieces. The rules also fixed the maximum size of the pieces, and specified that the statuettes and pots which were to accompany princes were to be drawn from the stocks of the 'Imperial Department of Model Makers'.

This ruling cannot have been enough to curb extravagance. We are told that later a strong complaint was lodged with the Imperial Household by a bureaucrat in the Ministry of Finance criticising in no uncertain terms the ostentation displayed in funeral ceremonies and the enormous expense involved. He did not scruple to include princes and grandees in his condemnation, though the *nouveaux riches* came in for most of the blame, and he enumerated the practices which caused the unprecedented squandering. First among these was the habit of displaying and then burying with the dead 'remarkably beautiful effigies of horses and men'. Apart from this bureaucrat's sedulousness and pedantry, the statement does reveal that the objects we of the present day admire so much were also considered beautiful by their contemporaries. Yet this man did not confine himself to fruitless criticism and condemnation. He had one very practical suggestion to make: to issue an edict whereby the mourners may not even parade the effigies through the streets, let alone display them in the pavilions, 'many of them eighty feet high'. If they really meant to do no more than express their filial piety by procuring solace to their dear departed, let the mourners proceed directly to the grave with their furnishings and there quickly dispose them around the dead. It is not known whether this sagacious suggestion was accepted by the emperor, but it is generally believed that the extravagant fashion ran out long before the end of T'ang, and that therefore most of the art of the T'ang potter which has come down to us dates from before the ninth century.

It is interesting to compare these customs with the earlier use of pottery as a substitute for human sacrifice from which they derive. The development matches

XX CAMELEER. *62 cm. high. The large eyes, the pronounced nose and ears, the intense look proclaim this menial person to be a foreigner, a Scythian or a Turk, though the garment is Persian. It has been established that Persian dress influenced not only the fashions of China but also those of most peoples of Asia contemporary to Sassanian Iran. This man, leading a camel-load of wares, is bound for the wealthy markets of T'ang China, across one or the other branch of the Silk Road. These figures accompanied camels into the tombs, modelled in proportion. The size of this specimen indicates the existence of pottery camels larger than any generally known.*
Collection Mrs Marika Prodan, Rome

the evolutionary cycle and gives a measure of the stage of civilisation at which T'ang had arrived which is not invalidated by certain grisly displays by contemporary neighbours or those conquerors of China, not long since barbarians, who had performed human sacrifices to the dead all along.

Now and again in the recent past the cruel practices of the barbarians had prompted emulation in one or two Chinese princes who were in a position to indulge their own ghosts. The *Li Chi* has this to tell about a Chinese prince of pre-Han times: 'As Chen Kan Shi was lying ill he assembled his male kin and addressed his son Tsun Chi thus: "When I am dead you must make my coffin large and cause my two concubines to lie in it with me, one on each side".' One might imagine that he meant his women-folk to be placed near him after their natural death, so that they could all be found lying next to each other as the Ming emperor Wan Li was found in recent archaeological excavations, but the quotation continues thus: 'When the father died the son said: "To bury the living with the dead is contrary to propriety. How much more so must it be to bury them in the same coffin." Accordingly he did not put the two ladies to death.' Obviously, the custom was already out of fashion before Han. Another annotation in the Classics tells of a general's father being especially fond of one of his concubines who had remained childless. Taken very ill, he first told his son to see that she remarried. But at the point of death he changed his mind and ordered that she be buried alive in the same grave with him. The *Tso Chuan* on the other hand tells us that the prince of Ch'u, in the year 528 B.C., twenty-three years before Confucius' birth, was visiting the house of one of the royal functionaries. Overcome by some despair which the chronicler does not care to investigate, the royal personage strangled himself. In order to do him honour the functionary killed two of his own daughters and buried them with the dead prince.

That such events should have happened in, and, for all we know, after, an era of such enlightenment as that of the great philosophers of China may be a shocking revelation. But if one remembers the Indian practice of suttee, which was abolish-

XXI HORSE WITH RIDER. *38 cm. high. Unglazed. This is sufficient proof that fine pieces were also made in unglazed pottery, as can be seen in many of the examples illustrated in black-and-white. This plate is also meant to provide a better understanding of the hue of most of the unglazed pieces. The orange-vermilion pigment on the rider, of which only traces have remained, is the more common a freddo colouring on such unglazed pieces; its particular intensity has always been a gauge by which dealers have tried to judge the authenticity of a piece. The breaks that are here clearly visible on the horse's legs — as well as breaks at the neck of figures, at protruding arms, at the tail of horses — are described as 'classical', a felicitous way of declaring that similar breaks are common, inevitable almost, on fragile objects which, even though they spent eleven centuries underground, have had to endure many vicissitudes between the time they were made and the time they reached the foreign markets. Collection H. E. Giovanni Gronchi, Rome*

ed only with the advent of British rule, it is not so surprising. Also, it should be considered that the fact that these events should be chronicled at all is evidence of their rarity and of the dismay they must have caused. There is little doubt that there was a continuous struggle between the barbarism of outsiders (and of indigenous memories) and the comparative enlightenment of the Chinese, formed by Confucius, Motzu, Chaungtzu, the scholarly and religious moderators who have always set the pace in China, sometimes even in opposition to their own princes.

Some scholars prefer to believe that the barbarians who came into contact with China and ruled there during some periods indulged in human sacrifice because they wanted to outdo the Chinese who, from time immemorial, had buried their dead with effigies, perishable at first, imperishable later. But did the barbarians never indulge in such brutality on their own initiative elsewhere? One cannot ignore the finds at Anyang which prove conclusively that the princes of that locality had their tombs sealed with earth wetted with the blood of the freshly slaughtered body-guard whose helmeted skulls were found in the paste itself. This was the practice in Shang-Yin and early Chou times, roughly from the fifteenth to the tenth century B.C., the very age whose manners Confucius chose as the model for his ethics. It is impossible to say whether the venerated sage knew the facts, but it is certain that if he did, he performed a remarkable piece of editing. We have in the annals more than one shocked pronouncement against the practice of human sacrifice.

There is other evidence to corroborate the suspicion that the barbarians committed ritual murder simply because they remained uncivilized longer than the Chinese. In China animal sacrifice persisted until Buddhism forbade it and long after. The rites contained complete vade-mecums for the would-be sacrificer, as we shall see later. And it is further recorded that a hundred years before Confucius a prince bent on an auspicious voyage had to crush a live dog under his chariot before setting out, while much later four dogs had to be slaughtered at each of the four city gates to keep the plague from coming through.

26 PRANCING HORSE. 42½ cm. high. Unglazed pottery covered with white slip and with traces of red painting on the trappings. *Seattle Art Museum.*

27 SEATED LADY. 14½ cm. high. Three-colour glazes over a white body. The lady is putting on make-up, looking at herself in one of the highly polished bronze mirrors so often found in tombs from the Late Chou period down to the T'ang and post-T'ang era. *Victoria and Albert Museum, London.*

28 FIGURE OF AN ACTOR. 38¾ cm. high. Unglazed pottery covered with white slip and with traces of painting. (See plate 7). *Seattle Art Museum.*

29 FIGURE IN ARMOUR. Unglazed pottery with traces of pigment. Although the armour is of Persian inspiration, similar helmets were buried in Shang-Yin tombs two thousand years earlier. *Collection J. Ritchie Esq., London.*

30 STANDING LADY. Red pottery with traces of unfired pigments over white slip. *Victoria and Albert Museum, Eumorfopoulos Collection, London.*

31 TWO MUSICIANS ON HORSEBACK. Unglazed white body with traces of pigment painting. *Collection J. Ritchie, Esq., London.*

32 FIGURE OF A MAN FEEDING A BIRD. Unglazed red pottery with traces of white slip and pigment decoration. *Collection John Nowell, Esq., London.*

33 FIGURE OF A MAN BEARING A BIRD. 39 cm. high. Unglazed red pottery with traces of white slip and pigment decoration. *Collection Hagedorn, Hamburg.*

34 FIGURE OF A WOMAN. 36 cm. high. Unglazed red pottery with traces of white slip and pigment decoration. *Collection Hagedorn, Hamburg.*

35 PAIR OF TOMB GUARDIANS. 20 cm. high. Thick ivory glaze over a white body. The costume is of Persian inspiration, but the faces are Mongolian. *Collection Mr and Mrs Victor Murray, London.*

36 GENTLEMEN AT THE HUNT. 38 cm. high. Unglazed grey pottery covered

with white slip. The garb of these two falconers is Persian, but the hats they wear are Turkish. *Collection Dr Ernst Hauswedell, Hamburg.*

37 GIANT FIGURE OF A FEMALE ATTENDANT. 110 cm. high. Unglazed buff pottery with traces of white pigment and fine green, black and red decorations. The size must have prompted the sculptor to execute the sleeves in an unsure and uncharacteristic manner. *British Museum, London.*

38 PAIR OF COURT LADIES. 37½ cm. high. Unglazed earthenware with traces of white slip and fine painted decoration. *Seattle Art Museum.*

39 FEMALE ATTENDANT. 28 cm. high. Unglazed red pottery. Though roughly finished – the joints of the two pieces from the mould are clearly visible here, too – maidenly grace and seriousness are well rendered in this less exalted specimen. *Collection Hagedorn, Hamburg.*

40 LOKAPALA. 70 cm. high. Yellow, green and cream glazes over a white body. A tomb protector at one of the cardinal points, this representation is derived from a Buddhist deity half man and half animal. The costume is that worn by army officers of the period. *Collection Mrs H. J. Heinz II.*

41 SEATED FIGURE OF A WOMAN HOLDING A GOOSE. 36 cm. high. Three colour glazes over a white body, the face unglazed. *Collection Comm. Corrado Zingone, Rome.*

42 FEMALE FIGURE BEARING A BIRD. 32 cm. high. Unglazed pottery painted with red, orange and black pigments on a white body. *Collection Mrs Richard E. Fuller, Seattle.*

43 CHILD. 12 cm. high. Unglazed red pottery. The visible mould joints place this piece among the mass-produced objects made for the poorer deceased. Interest is in the endeavour of the potter to present a Western type, perhaps the apprentice to some Mediterranean merchant. *T. Y. King, Jr, Hongkong.*

44 FEMALE DANCER. 16¼ cm. high. Unglazed grey pottery with white slip and traces of unfired pigment decoration. *British Museum, London.*

45 FIGURE OF BOY WITH PUPPY. Unglazed buff pottery with white pigment. *British Museum, Eumorfopoulos Collection, London.*

46 DANCING GIRL. 20½ cm. high. Unglazed pottery covered with white slip and traces of black and red pigments. The exaggerated length of the sleeves is pure caricature. *Collection Professor Roberto Ago, Rome.*

47 and 48 TWO BOXERS OR WRESTLERS. 10½ cm. high. Unglazed red pottery with traces of white slip and pigments. Another attempt to represent Western foreigners. *Collection H. E. Baron Jo van der Elst, Brussels.*

49 FIGURE OF A HORSEMAN. 26¼ cm. high. Light cream glaze over a white body. *Victoria and Albert Museum, London.*

26

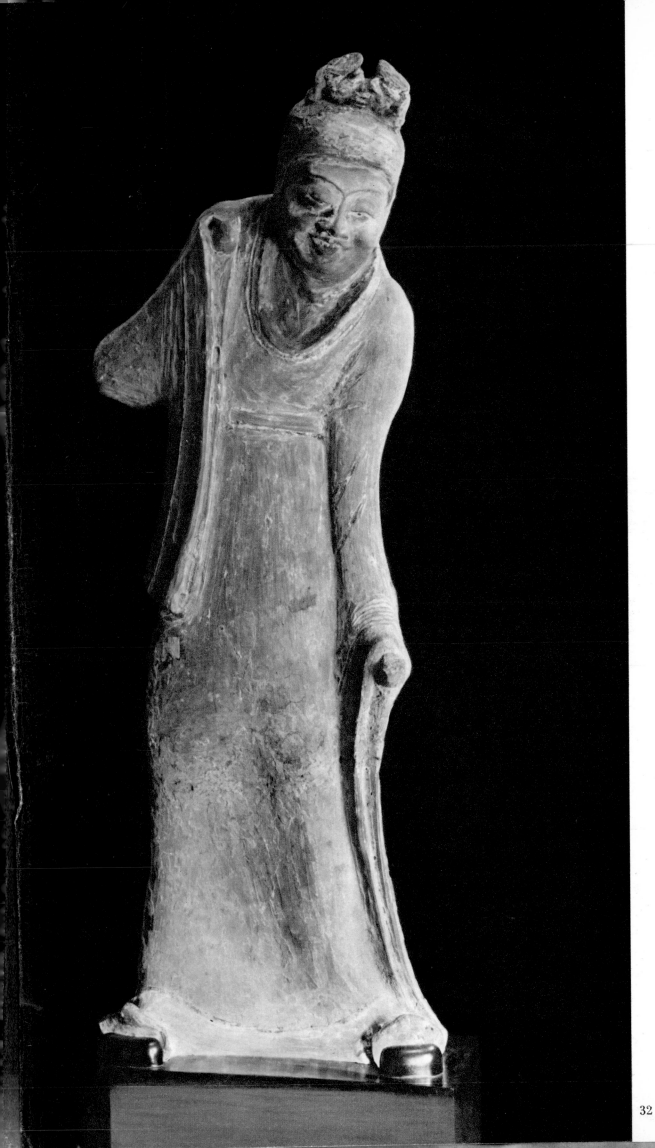

34

37

38

39

42

44

47

MING CH'I was the name given by the Chinese to the objects placed in tombs for the solace and use of the departed. An exact translation is difficult; a French savant once devoted an entire article to the effort to discover one. *Ming* means 'bright' but has overtones that bring it into the sphere of the 'sacred' – and, all things pertaining to the dead are, of course, sacred. It is important to note here as elsewhere in this introduction that *ming ch'i* (*ch'i* is best translated by the word 'accoutrement') and *ming ch'i* alone denotes the entire pre-Ming pottery from inside China; for as far as we know all surviving pottery came out of tombs.

Food and furniture for a ghost

Where were these tombs found? Where were the objects made? We will try to answer – or explain why one cannot fully answer – these questions before we go deeper into the dark world which the Chinese built for their dead.

The vast majority of the material now in foreign collections and museums comes from dealers in Peking and Shanghai who bought the objects from couriers from the interior without asking many questions. The trade was both illicit and dangerous, the province of renegades who had liberated themselves from age-old customs. '*Honan laide*' – 'come from Honan' – the dealer would say as part of his effort to entice the buyer. And the buyer would look knowing, pretending to some intelligence derived from careful study in Western universities and museums – but really knowing only that complicated exercises were needed to get the things out of China. As far as is known in the West (until the present Chinese government divulges the history of their recent considerable finds) dark grey clay figures and pots come from and were made in Shansi; white clay ware in Honan; red clay in Szechuan; cream or yellowish white in Ch'ang-sha. The recent appearance in the United States of a range of exquisite T'ang pottery reputedly dug up in the province of Shensi shows how tentative this scheme really is.

To go to the Chinese historians for information regarding kilns in T'ang times is an unrewarding task. Even on porcelain or porcellaneous stoneware the indications are vague and untrustworthy, and pottery must have been considered unworthy of the chronicler's interest for in the literature there is no direct mention of it at all.

Bound up with these problems of provenance is the equally serious one of dating. Whatever progress has been made here is due to three fairly complete groups of objects which were found together with burial tablets bearing dates. The first, from the tomb of a great soldier and administrator, the Chancellor Liu T'ing-hsün, bears the date of the 16th day of the 8th month of the 16th year of the K'ai-yüan era, corresponding to our A.D. 728, the day of T'ing-hsün's death in his 72nd year. A descendant of a family which had held important rank for over seven hundred years, the general had a reputation for dealing with enemies with the same ease with which he brushed flies from his face. His grave was found to contain beautiful, large glazed figures which before the discovery had been thought to appear only after the eighth century. The other two dated groups are from the tomb of General Yang, buried in A.D. 693, and from that of a prince by the name of Wen Shou-ch'eng who died in 683, in Loyang. The figures found in these tombs are very fine (those of General Yang are now in the Toronto museum), most of them measuring 30 and more inches in height.

But even the evidence of the inscribed tablets would not have satisfied western scientific discipline had it not been cross-checked by some remarkable finds of Chinese pottery made several thousand miles west, in Mesopotamia. Here, in the city of Samarra, which existed for not more than half a century, from 836 to 883, Chinese pottery was used or traded in, and remains were found in the course of archaeological excavations earlier in this century. The Samarra finds were meant for use and were therefore more highly fired and more thoroughly glazed, but otherwise they and the *ming ch'i* are alike. Another piece of reliable evidence is a fantastic repository in Japan, in Nara, the Shōsōin, where a devoted Japanese empress who lived in the T'ang period assembled the treasures which her late husband had imported from China. It has given most useful information not only to those interested in pottery, but to all students of T'ang history, art, literature and music, for it contains all the imperishable manifestations of those achievements in that great era.

It may be useful here to inform the reader of the present location of material for comparative study and such scholarly works which provide as much inform-ation as is possible under the circumstances described. Apart from the recent finds

XXII VESSEL IN THE FORM OF A DUCK. *32 cm. long. Keen observation of the things in nature has helped and not inhibited this tour de force. The special roundness of a duck's body becomes a harmonious vessel shape, and the arched neck a graceful handle almost as original as the one at the other end, the duck's curly tail. The observed colours are translated into glazes, the running of one into the other a satisfying reproduction of the behaviour of feathers.*

Collection Mr Avery Brundage, Chicago

in China due to industrial works and systematic archaeological excavations (a recent publication gives an insight into the quantities found in Sian-fu alone) and presumably displayed in or near the sites in which the objects were found, the largest collections of *ming ch'i* are now on the American continent, in the United States and Canada. The Royal Ontario Museum, under the curatorship of Bishop W. C. White, has assembled a magnificent group of T'ang pottery figures; and the Seattle Museum, thanks to the munificence of Dr and Mrs Fuller, possesses a collection put together only relatively recently and therefore highly selective. Other fine collections are in the W. R. Nelson Gallery of Art in Kansas City; at the Museum of Fine Arts in Boston; the Metropolitan Museum of New York; the Chicago Art Institute; the Pennsylvania University Museum, Philadelphia; and the Minneapolis Art Institute. In Europe, Britain boasts the famous Eumorfopoulos Collection which, just before the death of that pioneer and scholar, was divided between the British Museum and the Victoria and Albert Museum. A good, carefully selected range of T'ang pottery is at the City Art Gallery in Bristol, and many fine pieces are in private collections such as those of Mr and Mrs Desmond Gure in London and Sir Alan and Lady Barlow in Wendover. In Scandinavia, the Kunstindustri Museum, Copenhagen, the National Museum, Stockholm, and Dr Gustaf Lindberg in Norrköping possess some very interesting specimens; while the Museum für Kunst und Gewerbe in Hamburg has a larger collection than any of the other German museums. In France, the Musée Guimet and the Cernuschi, both in Paris; and in Italy, apart from the private collections mentioned in the notes accompanying the illustrations, the Istituto del Medio ed Estremo Oriente in Rome has a small but attractive selection.

This is perhaps the place to explain the criterion that governed the selection and arrangement of the illustrations in this book. As the text will bear out, an attempt has been made to present to a wider public artistic productions so far known to only a few collectors, students and art lovers. But, to satisfy these collectors and students as well, the colour reproductions not only present the most beautiful specimens (or at least the most beautiful specimens in the compiler's opinion) but also (and indeed mostly) such pieces as are not yet known to collectors

XXIII   TOMB GUARDIAN IN THE COSTUME OF A DIGNITARY. *65 cm. high. These are frequent inhabitants of tombs. The brilliant colour and the fine incised decoration on the carefully moulded breastplate make this specimen representative of the finer quality pieces, executed most probably by the court ateliers. The type portrayed is described by scholars as Caucaso-Iranian, because of the features, so different from those of the Chinese, the Semite or the Armenian. The race-guessing game becomes intricate when it is necessary to distinguish Khotanese from Altaic types, Tocharian from Mongols, Western Turks from Uighur Turks, mostly in Persian clothes and under one guise or another – soldier, dignitary, groom, mountebank or merchant – who inhabit the tombs of the T'ang dead.*

Collection Marchese G. F. Giaquili-Ferrini, Florence

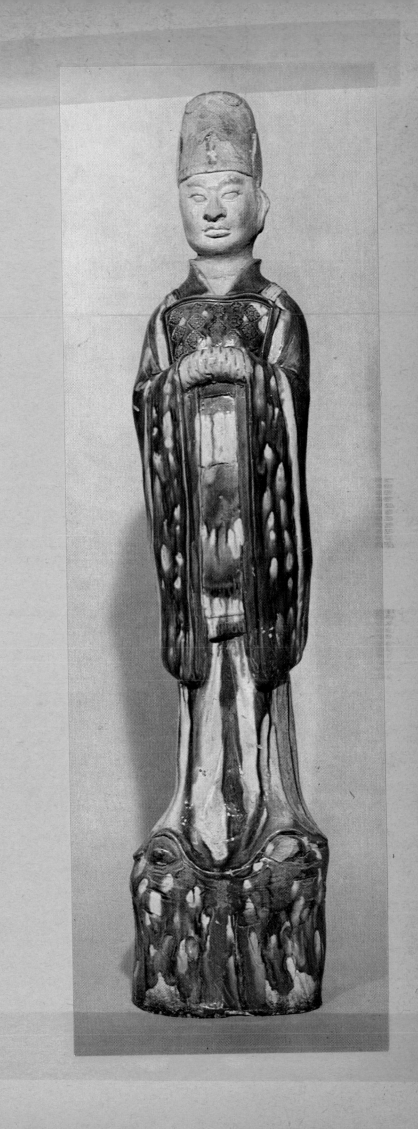

and students since they have only recently been discovered. This is also true of the black-and-white illustrations, though here the neophyte has been catered for more specifically and many pieces already known to experts, having been variously published and shown in exhibitions, are included. No work of this kind can be completely successful. The writer begs the indulgence of the more knowledgeable reader and, in extenuation of any possible inadequacies or mistakes of emphasis, pleads his affection for each of the pieces he has chosen to show. Perhaps a word must also be said about those of his judgments which the scholar may regard as personal or even arbitrary. They are based on the meagre 'scientific' knowledge we have (W. B. Honey's incomparable *The Ceramic Art of China and Other Countries of the Far East* is able to devote only three pages to this important development and deviation in Chinese ceramic art) and on conclusions matured in twenty years of contact and concern with T'ang pottery in Peking at a time (the thirties and forties) when most, certainly the finest, pieces passed through the locality.

* * *

The sacrificial handbooks referred to earlier state that nothing will so sustain the *kuei* of a person of rank as venison; while for the *kuei* of a secondary bureaucrat a few carps and tortoises will be quite enough. They also make it quite clear that there is a considerable gap between 'large victims' (horses and oxen) which are only slaughtered before the battle or, in funerary ceremonies, for the solace of important military corpses, and 'small victims' (sheep, pigs, fowl and fish). Fish and hare and broth made from dog meat is excellent for the *shen* – all of which necessitates a brief excursion into Chinese metaphysics.

According to these, man has two souls – the soul he is born with, and the soul that matures slowly after birth. The first, which in the living man is called *p'o*, is a particle of the earth, like the element *Yin* in the eternal Chinese scheme. The second, called *hun* in the living, is instead a particle of heaven, the element *Yang*. In terms of energy, *p'o* belongs to the sperm and *hun* to the breath. After death, both survive, though they change their name, *p'o* becoming *kuei* and *hun* becoming *shen*. But both maintain their vitality, are sped on to their finality, through food and drink, as they did in life – enjoying greatly any extra sacrifice that the living may wish to make to them. They, in return, speak well of the living

XXIV   LARGE HORSE. *80 cm. high. The types of horses portrayed by the T'ang potter-sculptors varied greatly because the vogue for the animal in T'ang times created a flow into China from many parts of the world – from Mongolia, Persia, Bactria and Arabia. Appreciation of the horse coincided with the pressure exerted on China by the horse-cultures of Central Asia, which culminated eventually with the Mongol conquest three hundred years later. The florid trappings often found on these animals are a Persian vogue. It does not appear before T'ang times. Size, condition and the brilliant caramel colour of the saddle-cloth are the unusual features of this imposing piece of sculpture.*   Collection T. Y. King, Jr, Hongkong

to the powers of the other world whose ear they naturally have; and if the means for their subsistence are not forthcoming they punish the living by not only slandering them in high places, but returning to earth to get food and drink themselves; subsist they must, subsisting being their chief function. In this effort they become noisy and even harmful. In cases where the deceased has died before his time, the *p'o* (now the *kuei*) is not mature enough to turn back into the earth in which he should dwell and so wanders, a ghost. The *kuei* always creates trouble, the celestial *shen* being presumably less concerned with mundane matters. The term *kuei* is current with the Chinese even today. They use it to define foreigners, for instance, to manifest their dislike for them in the expression *yang kuei* – 'overseas spirit of the earth' – which has always been translated as 'foreign devil', not too far-fetched a rendering, for the word *kuei* does in fact include notions of Hades, of a subterranean, mischievous after-life.

It is not easy to give this religion a name. It is certain, however, that Taoism endorsed this indigenous, age-old belief, by attaching it to the Yin and Yang principle and adding the specification that most souls in the end vanish, disintegrate, 'return into the Great Wall', except for an élite, the identity of which it is not in truth difficult to guess – the Taoist genii, which go on for ever. The Buddhists themselves, after they came to China, had to take these early Chinese beliefs into account. In explaining their laws governing metempsychosis they made full use of the *kuei* and *shen* terminology. It was only about the beginning of T'ang, with a more robust assertion of their creed, that the twin souls were made to go through the Buddhist hell before coming out of it reincarnated.

To return to the indigenous Chinese ideas about souls, however; it must be noted that the bereaved knew exactly what was good for them. Each of the two souls had its particular craving. The *kuei*, inferior and earthy, is partial to coins, and as long as it gets them is pleased to remain underground, his home. The *shen*, superior, sups of the effluvia from wine and grains before it departs to heavenly quarters. Earth for one and heaven for the other, these are the ends they yearn for because the dead will find peace only when the Yin and Yang are separated. All of life is an interaction, an intimacy between the two principles. Death, true death, is achieved only when the two are truly separated. When this is procured, the living are not only relieved of the interference of the dead but transcendentally benefited by their goodwill. The tomb accessories – coins, vessels for food and drink, effigies in substitution of real sacrificial material – are placed in the grave to this end.

Scholarly opinion has differed on the real meaning of the clay statuary. Regarding the reproductions of animals, many assume that they replace real ones at the instigation of Buddhism even more than of economy. Regarding the human effigies, others believe that they are in origin connected with a variety of black magic whereby part, at least, of the qualities of the effigied person remains attached to the statuette. On the other hand, paper money is burned today to satisfy the *kuei*, together with paper servants, horses, carts and even motorcars. The dead, thus possessing the effigies of those who were their chattels and vassals, maintain their power over them and can use them as hostages to see that the care and offerings which are their due are properly given. Still another school of thought inclines towards the belief that the reproductions are a symbolic assurance of the living to the dead that they, the dead, go on participating in the ownership of the chattels and persons they have left behind. A habit which survives to this day in China is quoted in support of this theory also. In Amoy, on the day of the winter solstice, women make paste statuettes of chickens, pigs or dogs which have been born from the animals left in legacy by the deceased, and offer them symbolically at his grave.

Whatever the truth – and in that twilit Chinese vagueness which occidentals will never understand, all three assumptions may well be true – all that accompanied the corpse in the grave was a price paid by the living so that they should be left in peace: a notable facet of ancestor worship. Whether this was the outcome of some ethical intention of the humanist moderators who have always governed the Chinese mind (a wise manipulation of the Cruel Father complex latent in every primitive culture) it is difficult to say. We do know, however, that Confucius encouraged ancestor worship and that if he perhaps the least metaphysical of all philosophers, did so, it can only have been with ethical ends in view. It is certain that this awe, this veneration for ancestors, bore abundant moral fruit. It called from the young respect (a sentiment most enduringly stimulated by fear) for the aged because their proximity to ancestorhood made of them a power-to-be; and it induced from the old approaching death, a sort of sainthood, exemplary behaviour, righteousness in judgment, and dignity. For a people as lively as the Chinese, whose chief preoccupation has always been with their own survival, this was an important covenant.

50 CAMEL. 82½ cm. high. Cream, green and yellow glazes over a white body. This animal was first brought to China by the Persians. It has been imposs- ible to establish the meaning of the strange ogre's mask which is so often found on the pack of these T'ang camels. *British Museum, London.*

51 DWARF CARRYING A PACK. 22½ cm. high. Unglazed white pottery with traces of black and red pigments. *British Museum, London.*

52 LION SEATED ON ROCKS. 23 cm. high. Thin transparent cream glaze with silvery iridescence covering a white body. *Royal Ontario Museum, Toronto.*

53 HORSE. 27½ cm. high. Blue splashes on a cream glaze covering a white body. The turn of the head gives this animal its vitality. *British Museum, London.*

54 HORSE. 72½ cm. high. Cream, green and caramel glazes over a white body. This Bactrian animal is adorned with Sassanian bronze plaques and with a saddle-cloth which is given an unusual wind-swept effect. It is included to illustrate the great variety of horses that were bred in and brought to T'ang China from Khotan, Mongolia and the Western Pamirs. *Royal Ontario Museum, Toronto.*

55 HEAD OF A MAN. 16½ cm. high. This fragment, wearing a sort of Phrygian bonnet like the actor in Plate 68, was excavated in Shensi Province. *Shensi Provincial Museum, Sian-fu.*

56 LION BITING HIS PAW. 12½ cm. high. Light tan glaze over a white body. *Seattle Art Museum.*

57 SEATED FEMALE DANCER. 16½ cm. high. Unglazed white pottery with traces of red, black and white pigments. Western influence in dress is strong, a complete departure from the flowing robe previously worn by Chinese women. *Collection Mr and Mrs Charles Fix, Athens.*

58 FEMALE ATTENDANT WITH VOLUMINOUS SKIRT. 20 cm. high. Thick ivory glaze over a white body. The heavy potting and the exaggerated skirt place this figure into a later T'ang than the more elegantly potted Kuchā women wearing the same head-dress in Plate VII. *Collection Mr and Mrs Victor Murray, London.*

59 PAIR OF FEMALE ATTENDANTS. 18 cm. high. Green glaze over a buff pottery with traces of pigment and gilding. Sui or early T'ang dynasty. *Grand Rapids Art Gallery, Grand Rapids, Michigan.*

60 HORSE. 68 cm. high. Unglazed white pottery with traces of pigment. This fine Bactrian animal bears features reminiscent of Greek horses sculpted in stone. *Collection Dr Alessandro Campilli, Rome.*

61 OX. Unglazed pottery covered with white slip and with traces of red pigment. The trappings are probably part of the panoply of animal sacrifice. *British Museum, Eumorfopoulus Collection, London.*

62 TOMB GUARDIAN. $102\frac{1}{2}$ cm. high. Unglazed white earthenware painted and decorated with unfired pigments. *Victoria and Albert Museum, London.*

63 STANDING LADY. 37 cm. high. Unglazed red pottery with white slip and traces of red and black pigments. *Victoria and Albert Museum, London.*

64 HORSE. 57 cm. high. Unglazed white body with the saddle pigmented in greens, yellows and cream. *Seattle Art Museum.*

65 PAIR OF TOMB GUARDIANS. 90 cm. high. The costumes are those of court dignitaries, the shoes of Persian design; and the expression fear-inspiring, a deterrent against evil spirits. *Collection Edward H. Weiss, Chicago.*

66 THREE SERVANTS MADE OF LEAD. $16\frac{1}{2}$ cm. high. The influence of pottery on these three figures found in a T'ang tomb is quite obvious. Such lead figures are very rare. *Istituto per il Medio ed Estremo Oriente, Rome.*

67 SLEEPING PIG. $10\frac{1}{2}$ cm. long. An important and also beloved member of the Chinese economy from earliest times. *Shensi Provincial Museum, Sian-fu.*

68 AN ACTOR. 49 cm. high. The histrionic expression is vividly brought out. This figure, like those in Plates 67 and 69, and the fragment in Plate 55, was excavated in Shensi Province. *Shensi Provincial Museum, Sian-fu.*

69 SEATED COURT LADY. $28\frac{1}{2}$ cm. high. Glazed. *Shensi Provincial Museum, Sian-fu.*

70 LION. 25 cm. high. Green and cream glazes over a white body. Lions were not indigenous to China. Embassies from Persia and Arabia brought specimens as presents to the Chinese court. The lion in Chinese art is, however, inspired mainly by its frequent representation in Persian art. *British Museum, London.*

71 TWO POLO PLAYERS ON HORSEBACK. 31 cm. long. Unglazed red pottery with traces of white, red and black pigments. *Barling of Mount Street, Ltd., London.*

72 TWO HORSES. 55 cm. high. Dark caramel and greenish-white glazes over a white body. Runnels down the length of the neck and a hole at the base of the tail suggest that real horse hair was inserted to give the animal a more life-like appearance. *Collection Dr Umberto Ortolani, Rome.*

53

55

56

59

62

65

67

68

69

71

72

WHILE THE VESSELS found in the tombs proclaim their particular functions by their shapes – wide mouths are grain containers and narrow mouths were meant to contain wine and spirits – the earthenware figures found in the tombs need closer examination before we can understand exactly what they represent.

To those acquainted with the Chinese it may have occurred that many of the human types portrayed by the T'ang sculptor-potter are not indigenous to his country. To students of Chinese dress this anomaly is glaring, though it can be explained by the Classics, the historians of T'ang, who acquaint us with the great interest in foreigners during that period. Already in Han, China was an expansionist power even more fascinated by foreign ways, even less isolationist than Rome. We find in the annals a pronouncement attributed to the emperor Ling (168-188): that occidental costume, furniture, food and music is much admired and loved by him. If we consider that these were the years of both Han and Roman expansion we may surmise that the emperor's general term 'occidental' may well have included Rome – a compliment returned by Rome, as Pliny tells us in his letters, when he complains of the high cost of silk from China which was used to give more subtlety to the Roman matrons.

We have archaeological evidence of the influence of foreign dress from sculptures earlier than T'ang, depicting in bas-relief battles between Chinese and western barbarians. The enemy is always portrayed wearing a sort of Phrygian cap, the same that is so frequently worn in T'ang as to become a sort of male uniform. To proceed with male dress, the high-toed shoes worn by officials, probably exaggerated in the statuary, were the *dernier cri* at the beginning of the seventh century. They were first made of leather, later of cloth, when they were universally worn to the end of T'ang. The greatest care was given to the manufacture of these shoes and the whole industry held an important rank in the artisan world of that period.

There is no doubt that these shoes were of foreign origin, even if the Persians who wore them only did so to cross the desert that separated their home from the

Plate 35

Plates 62, 65

125

Chinese trading centres. Historians of T'ang inform us that the capital city of Ch'ang-An provided a great spectacle of foreign dress, customs and manners. Though the Chinese have always insisted on referring to all foreigners as barbarians (so that one wonders whether the word can have as grim a meaning for them as it has for us), there is much more evidence than that provided by the burial figurines to suggest that they were not indifferent to their influence and charm. An edict of the emperor T'ai Tsung is not only a revelation of the cosmopolitan flavour of those times but also a reminder of the great curiosity of the T'ang Chinese. The order requested that court painters go out and faithfully depict the outlandish people who thronged the caravanserais of the capital, their ways and their customs. In these colonies, particular inns catered to the tastes of the 'barbarians'; so that while one specialised in the fat-tailed mutton so dear to the gluttonous Turkomans, another cooked puppy meat to delight the palate of the ambassador from Sinlo.

Though the silk trade between Rome and China had long ceased, the Byzantines, or 'East Romans' as they were called by the Chinese, sent several envoys to the T'ang capital. Certainly, the barrier between the two civilised peoples had been increased by the Central Asian baronial toughs who exacted tax and 'managed' the hazardous task of transportation; yet each nation knew of the other. While a Byzantine writer of the sixth century gives an awed account of the great Far Eastern empire, we know from the Chinese annals that the emperor of the day, T'ai Tsung, was entertaining an ambassador from Constantinople (called Fu Lin by the Chinese) who had brought him a rich present; and that after further embassies in 667 and 711, a group of 'priests of great virtue' arrived at the court of Ch'ang-An in 742.

Not infrequent among the foreign types found within the figurines which adorn the T'ang tombs, is one distinctly semitic. He has striking features – a hooked nose, thick lips and the large eyes which in fact grace all the more occidental types portrayed. He is often depicted carrying a pack on his back and wearing a felt hat coming to a point, a Persian borrowing. We know that Jews settled in China and that at Kaifengfu until recently there existed a colony which continued to worship in synagogues, to wear a lock of hair in front of each ear and fill bureaucratic posts, rather than practise trade. However, traders they must originally have been, for synagogues are known to have been established all along

Plate XXIX

Plate 83

XXV Jar with four handles. *16 cm. high. The roundness, completed rather than interrupted by the four handles, is an apt illustration of the potter's constant need to reproduce the forms of nature. Blue must have been costly or the most difficult colour to work with in the kiln for it is found less often than the other four colours, and is almost only present in the finer pieces. Cobalt, which gives a fine blue colour over a wide range of temperatures, must have been imported from Persia to obtain this glaze. Only later, in the Ming period, was it bartered directly by the Arabs and Turks for Chinese porcelain.* Seattle Art Museum

the Asiatic trade routes, where Jews probably assembled and rested in numbers great enough to constitute real settlements. Persian documents written in Hebrew exist to prove that the proselytising zeal of these dealers must have been considerable, for they confirm the existence in T'ang times of Judaized Persians. Another document has been found, written on paper in Hebrew. Paper was made only in China then, and it is obviously a letter written by a Jew residing there.

Plate 96

For a series of reasons, anthropological, historical, and even philological, a division is made between these semitic types. The main consensus of opinion tends to separate the Semites from what are called Armenoids — the Armenians from the Jews. It is curious that this should be the case since it is admitted that the Chinese must have been hard put to it to distinguish not only an Armenian from a Jew but both from an Arab. The classification is partly based on the costumes the types wear — though most of these seem to have adopted the Persian style of dress. The facial characteristics studied with such zeal may well be but the revelation of greater or lesser skill of the potter-sculptor; for it is much to expect an artist of so generally unscientific an inclination as the Chinese to become involved in the finer points of anthropology. However, it may be interesting to note that in the opinion of these experts, the more the nose looks like the beak of a bird of prey, the closer the type is to being Armenoid.

It is to Persia more than to any other country that the potter-sculptor of T'ang China looked in his creation of the foreign statuette. Apart from the representation of Persian dress on Chinese people, revealing its influence on the Chinese mode — an influence which Persia exerted equally over the greater part of Central Asia — distinctly Persian types are not infrequent. The Chinese knew them well. Traders in all sorts of commodities, from silver to cosmetics, from brocade to indigo, from soldiery to ideas, they shared important settlements in China proper with Arabs along the Grand Canal and the Yangtse river. Once, when Chinese help was refused the Persians, and they were overcome by the violent Arabs (for, politically, the two countries exchanged not only envoys but military help as well), a defeated prince was taken into the Chinese palace and appointed general in the Emperor's guard. Gaining in importance, the Persian general at last caused a Zoroastrian temple to be built in Ch'ang-An.

The most typical article of Persian male attire is the garment which can best be described as a tunic with a round neck. It reaches to the knees and is held tight

XXVI JAR WITH COVER. *20 cm. high. A mottled cover on a plain jar is unusual enough to put the relationship between the two under suspicion. But the intentional originality is revealed by the light streak of blue touched on to the jar's belly, proclaiming that the combination is not fortuitous. Such jars with a wide neck, with or without covers, were meant to contain cereals for the feeding of the more earthbound of the two souls which the Chinese believed inhabited the body and went on living after death (see page 100). Collection C. T. Loo et Cie, Paris.*

around the waist by a wide band of cloth or leather. On top, a long-sleeved garment, half-cape, half-coat, was thrown carelessly over the shoulders in a manner not unlike that of the European hussars of the last century. The long, pleated skirt is the Persian woman's favourite attire, accompanied by a high-waisted, long-sleeved blouse and a long scarf often draped over the head. Persian men wore

Plate 78
Plate 49

close-fitting trousers under the tunic, which were often tucked into boots reaching the knee. Riders and huntsmen wore 'chaps' like American cowboys, presumably made of leather. All of these purely Persian features were eventually adopted by the Chinese and by the peoples living near them – the Mongols, the Turks, and even the Jews and Armenians. Another feature which the Chinese copied from the Persians was chain-mail, used by the military of both nations.

But perhaps the greatest Persian impact on Chinese costume came in the form of the maquillage habit of Near Eastern women. Nothing describes it better than the protest registered by Po Chü-i, one of the great poets of T'ang:

Plates IX, XIV

'The current fashions started in the city and spread in all directions. No rouge is smoothed on the cheeks, nor are faces powdered. A dark ointment is put on the lips to make them look like mud, and both eyebrows are painted like *pa* [Chinese character meaning 8], painted very low. Everybody, whether light or dark, beautiful or ugly, ceased to be natural. After they had dolled themselves up they had a melancholy look, an air of sadness. The hair was dressed in a round top-knot without any side-locks, the *tui chi* fashion. The red "beauty marks" are so brilliant that they make them look as though they are always blushing. Please remember that the fashions of the Yüan-ho era [806 to 820], the splotched face and the piled-up hair, are not Chinese.'

Plate XX

The Turks, Western and Uighur, are also often found portrayed in T'ang pottery. In costume often undistinguishable from the Persians, there are some definite Turkish types, in most cases represented in the tombs as judges and guardians. These peoples had the closest contacts with the Chinese, as much in trade as in political matters. It was the Chinese who had been instrumental in dividing them so as to be in a position to annex later a large slice of the vast Turkish realm, eventually allowing the Chinese emperor to invade the territory of Samarkand.

In spite of the praiseworthy efforts of some scholars to classify the foreign types found in T'ang tombs, considerable confusion still prevails. It is certainly

XXVII SERVING MAIDS. *16 cm. high. Kneeling figures of this type are rarely glazed. The earth acids have attacked the green on some of the garments more than the other glazes because of its copper oxide content. 'Serving maid' is a guess for these two persons. The real status of the great number of women in the household of a rich Chinese gentleman has always been difficult to assess. It is interesting that the style of hairdress of these two figurines has been traced to the Near East.*
Collection Dr Eric Vio, Hongkong

not lessened by the existence in T'ang times of outlying centres where nations and races were incredibly mixed, like those in the Oasis of Turfan, for instance. Such purely commercial settlements comprised types from the Celtic to the Mongol, from the Latin to the Indian, using languages long since dead.

Plates xx, 35 The garb of grooms and servants is all foreign, as are the grooms and servants themselves. As early as the third century, retainers were recruited from prisoners of war. There are repeated references to them in the annals, perhaps as a modest variation on the theme of successful campaigns. One of the references gives details of the servants' menial duties and another reveals the reasons for the presence of groom effigies in such great number: 'At the reception of a foreign visitor or at a funeral service they [the prisoner-grooms] lead the horses to their appointed places on the meeting ground. They do the same when the consecrated horse is brought for the funeral sacrifice.' It also reveals, conclusively, that in those days the horse, as noble an animal for the Chinese as it has ever been for us, as we shall see, was slaughtered in sacrifice.

Plates xxiii, 40, 62, 65, 97 Other male figures found in T'ang tombs are dignitaries, officials, guardians and protectors of tombs. The presence of these originates in the wide practice of exorcism. They are meant to drive away morbid influences, and it is believed that the figures are portraits of living exorcists who walked in front of the funeral processions and were the first to enter the tomb where they performed their duties, ridding the abode of the dead of all evil influences before the coffin was placed in it. Some of the earthenware portraits of these important functionaries have Plate viii rotted wood remains in the holes where the hands joined. They carried wooden swords and lances with which they fought or kept at a respectable distance the evil spirits, for the Chinese have always seen evil in the guise of soldiers, soldiers that must be fought by soldiers. This is a belief that lasted till very recently. The time was not far off when servants would return from their homes in the country and recount deeds of supernatural valour performed by ghostly soldiers. After an Ovidian metamorphosis from peaceful trees into perfectly armed military, they fell upon the hapless Japanese garrison in the village and killed every man in it. Ghosts were evil, it was explained, but they were Chinese. In the T'ang tombs Plate xxxiii the armour soldiers wear is not in the T'ang fashion but a relic from previous times. It is intended as some sort of proof of the transcendent character of these mighty fighters of evil genii. The good ghost-soldiers not only protected the dead against the invisible spirits. Fortified by a hyperphysical aura in the mind of the

XXVIII   *Vase. 31 cm. high. This typical T'ang shape becomes the elegant but still forceful mei p'ing in the succeeding dynasty, the Sung. The glazes have been applied by a potter with the courage to let his abstract composition be completed with the help of nature's laws over flowing liquids. This technique was also experimented with on porcelain by K'ang Hsi potters, in the phase of 'San Ts'ai' which the Chinese call 'Tiger Skin'. Collection C. T. Loo et Cie., Paris*

Plate 77 living, it was hoped that they would also keep away tomb violators. That many of these soldiers have a western aspect can be explained by the fact that the Chinese armies were made up in part of foreign mercenaries, and foreigners are always much more dramatic than local people. In the hey-day of T'ang thousands of foreign soldiers settled with their families in Ch'ang-An, the capital.

The tombs also contained mountebanks, boxers, actors – effigies of the men who performed in the tents to delight the dead man's friends and procure the envy of his enemies. Dwarfs are often found. Not unlike the Spanish court in the late Renaissance, princes of the T'ang dynasty favoured these creatures. One of the T'ang emperors thought so highly of a dwarf that he appointed him examining magistrate.

The effigies of women are interesting because they reveal so much that tallies with our historical knowledge of that era. In no other period of China, perhaps in no period in the history of any people, has woman played such an important part, not only in the social state but in the political state as well. This may seem odd to those who consider the battle of the sexes settled only when polygamy is abolished and equal rights granted to both contenders. For though T'ang China was perhaps the most polygamous society the world has yet seen, everything would indicate that the reason for this was because woman was so intensely liked, her great ascendancy in that period being once again witness of the inevitable rapport between desire (demand) and acquiescence (supply).

In T'ang China one of the most enlightened rulers whom we have already mentioned as ministering to Buddhism was a woman, the Empress Wu, widow of the emperor Kao Tsung. Though disliked by her chroniclers, all Confucians, she was certainly a woman of great acumen and character since she was able to hold the reins of state for so long at so strenuous a moment of China's history. Another important conditioner of history of that period is Yang Kuei Fei, more completely a woman: successful concubine to two emperors – father and son – and ardent, she was not averse to changing the course of an empire in a fit of languor brought on by love-sickness. Apart from their political importance, both were great patronesses of the arts and of learning, free from religious prejudice, conscious of that most characteristic of T'ang qualities, its cosmopolitanism. These are attitudes

XXIX NEAR EASTERN MERCHANT. *38 cm. high. The object held by this figure is a skin sack. Portraits of foreign travellers to China are not unusual in the furnishings of T'ang tombs. They are mostly seen bearing gifts or trappings typical of their trade, or tending horses and camels. This one is probably bearing a skin full of wine from the Palestinian coast of the Mediterranean, though the marked nose resembling the beak of a bird of prey, the glaring eye and the widely separated eyebrows have convinced some scholars that this type is Armenoid rather than Jewish. The heavy beards and powerful noses of some of the travellers must have made a great impression on the Chinese so scantily provided by nature with either (see page 126).*
Seattle Art Museum

worth mentioning for they reveal traits uncommon in women, who tend to be conditioned to conformism and reverence for the *status quo*.

The T'ang dynasty saw important women painters, poets and calligraphers. But more than anything, it saw a great number of what must be called courtesans – young women who had since girlhood studied the art of pleasing and interesting men, including lessons in riding, falconry, music, poetry and polo-playing. Chroniclers of the age inform us that this extreme interest in woman, this desire to be continuously surrounded by them, is explained by a desire to imitate the habits of barbarian princes. It is more probable – though the importance of example must not be minimised – that this increase in female importance was no more than the outward mark of great prosperity. Monogamy came to Europe with the poverty of the Dark Ages and persists, with certain equivocal variations, in this era because the wealth, instead of going to the few, goes toward the levelling off of the classes. In China the number of wives has always been the most accurate indication of the husband's wealth – until Communism decreed that, at least as long as Five Year Plans shall last, each man shall have no more than one wife. In the T'ang period, however, there was only one and that a very brief reaction, prompted by religious principles, against excessive numbers of wives. A flood occurred. The diviners maintained that it was caused by an excess of the Yin principle, both female and appertaining to water. The harems were dismissed. One prince alone required two hundred coaches to cart the women away. When the flood was over, the coaches returned.

This joy in women is amply reflected in T'ang poetry and painting, but nowhere more than in the funerary ware with which we are here concerned. The love that has gone into the modelling is manifest in every line, revealing itself in re-creation of woman's dignity, of her grace, of her importance, without losing sight of her capacity for sweet foolishness. Dancers wear long sleeves. So dancers' sleeves are exaggerated in good humoured caricature. Why do dancers wear long sleeves? Because long sleeves are difficult to handle 'and only good dancers wear long sleeves', and only good dancers, of course, accompany the dead. Ssu-ma Chien, China's great historian, coins a proverb: 'She who has long sleeves is a good dancer, he who has much money is a good merchant.'

Every particular of woman's dress is observed and reproduced. She wears chignons at either side of her head – a foreign fashion which she has taken over. Or a tiara like a bird's wings, copied from the wives of Sassanid rulers of Persia now driven into China by the redoubtable Arabs. In one hand she bears a lotus flower, an influence of Buddhism. The tight sleeve, the hobble skirt, the long scarf worn shawl-like and falling down the front of the dress – all are fashions from abroad. Plump women who have passed their first youth seem to have been found the most worthy of immortality for we find them again and again, not only made of pottery in the tombs, but in paintings, in silver inlays on lacquer, in embroidery, more often than not in association with birds, trees and flowers.

Plates 44, 57

Plate XIV

Plate IX

Plate II

The pleasure that T'ang men had in women is almost equalled by the pleasure they had in horses. 'Autumn Mist' was the name of one of T'ai Tsung's six favourite chargers which accompanied him into battle. After death, immortalised in large stone bas-reliefs, they accompany the emperor into his tomb. They are rugged and powerful, these horses, indigenous to China; and they are hewn into the grey stone of Shensi by artists who must have loved the animals as much as the emperor himself. 'Autumn Mist' has been wounded in the chest by an arrow, which a faithful retainer, in the heat of battle, is trying to pull out of the beast, rigid with pain. No less beautiful are the stone horses, in the round, of emperor Kao Tsung's tomb, also in Shensi province. One of them is winged, a Chinese Pegasus. In poetry as much as in painting, the horse is exalted. The armies that have conquered the surrounding mounted barbarians have come to understand and to appreciate the animal and, themselves adopting cavalry with success, consider the beast worthy of honour. In this prosperous era, the horse converges on Ch'ang-An, the capital, from all corners of the globe. Poets and painters, sculptors and potters, pay him homage each in his own idiom. The delight taken in portraying the horse becomes an end in itself; the artist is concerned now only with the artistic possibilities offered by so noble, strong and graceful an animal. Women are made to mount them, so that the two can be considered together, thus introducing into China a fashion from Khotan. Studies of horses at full gallop prove that the Chinese artist did not in general choose to portray   Plate 71 static objects simply because he did not know how to deal with movement. Even religion takes up the horse, and transforms him, through frequent metamorphoses, into the dragon, that finest of all the Chinese zoomorphic inventions.

Camels occur frequently in T'ang tombs, often large in size and portrayed   Plates XII, 18, 20, 50 with great attention to detail. Some are burdened with produce, among which is often a large grotesque mask. There have been no suggestions as to the meaning of   Plate 50 this return of the *T'ao tieh*, the stylized mask found on the early bronzes. The insistent presence of the camels themselves is obscure, apart from their power of evoking that 'foreignness' so cherished in T'ang.

A shrewd combination of animal and man is achieved by the production of the twelve figurines representing the twelve years of the Chinese cycle. Their   Plates 84 - 95 presence in the tombs indicates a sort of sacrifice of time, on a metaphysical level, to the tutelary gods. Artistically, they often constitute a remarkable repository of human types. They seem clear proof that there are certain basic types which transcend the featural differences between the races. Who does not recognise among the figures on plates 84-95 a relative or a friend, if not indeed himself?

73 GROUP AROUND CART. 40 cm. high. Glazed white pottery in light caramel except for the faces and the bullock's muzzle. The nearer figure is a caricature of a foreign trader; the other is a Chinese attendant. *Seattle Art Museum.*

74 FIGURE OF A DANCER. 19¼ cm. high. Olive-green glaze over a white body. The costume and type is Khorezmian, a nomad people from the Siberian steppes. The posture is the same as that of Cossack dancers today. *Royal Ontario Museum, Toronto.*

75 TWO DWARFS. 11 cm. high. Unglazed red pottery with traces of white slip. *T. Y. King, Jr, Hongkong.*

76 CARAVAN MAN. 66 cm. high. Green, caramel and cream glazes over a white body, face unglazed. A figure very similar to this was found in the dated tomb of General Yang (93 A.D.). While the hat is identical with those worn by the Persians of the period, the man is of Caucasian type. *Collection Mrs Marika Prodan, Rome.*

77 WARRIOR. 43 cm. high. Unglazed pottery with traces of white, grey and red pigments. The armour worn by this tomb guardian is of established Persian origin. The peculiarity of the scales which are upside-down is common to many representations of armour in the T'ang period and before. Sui or early T'ang dynasty. *Royal Ontario Museum, Toronto.*

78 GROOM. 47 cm. high. Cream, green and yellow glazes over a white body. A man of Caucasian-Iranian type wearing another style of Persian hat. *Royal Ontario Museum, Toronto.*

79 SEMITIC TRAVELLER. 29 cm. high. Yellowish glaze on white pottery. The small ewer he carries is Persian. *Royal Ontario Museum, Toronto.*

80 FIGURE OF AN ACTOR. 28¾ cm. high. A dark green, almost black, glaze

providing the flesh tints, the odd curly hair and the scant costume lead us to assume this to be the portrait of an entertainer from Polynesia. *British Museum, London.*

81 WARRIOR ON HORSEBACK. 18 cm. high. Light cream glaze over a white body, with traces of red and black pigments over the glaze. The armour is from Persia – six hundred years later, the Crusaders will take inspiration from the same source. *British Museum, London.*

82 YOUTH WITH GRAECO-ROMAN FEATURES. 13¾ cm. high. Unglazed grey pottery with traces of pigments. *Royal Ontario Museum, Toronto.*

83 SEMITIC PEDLAR. 26 cm. high. Unglazed earthenware with traces of white slip. *Seattle Art Museum.*

84-95 TWELVE ZOOMORPHIC FIGURINES.
These represent the Chinese cycle of years.

Rat   (41.6 cm. high)   Ox   (42   cm. high)   Tiger   (38.9 cm. high)
Hare (39.3 cm. high)   Dragon (39.2 cm. high)   Serpent (41.7 cm. high)
Horse (39.7 cm. high)   Sheep (38.9 cm. high)   Monkey (39.7 cm. high)
Cock (41.2 cm. high)   Dog   (41   cm. high)   Pig   (41.2 cm. high)
Shensi Provincial Museum, Sian-fu.

96 FIGURE OF AN ARMENIAN. 36 cm. high. Three colour glazes over a white body. This figure is presented to stress the caricaturing intentions of the T'ang potter. *Royal Ontario Museum, Toronto.*

74

75

80

84

85

86

88

89

90

91

92

93

94

95

HAVING DEALT WITH the figurative representations in the earthenware tomb furniture of the T'angs, it is time to return to the vessels, to basic shapes, and to set them in their historical context, for surely the most important feature of the T'ang potter's production is the development – the establishment – of the final Chinese forms. With the beginning of T'ang, outside influences have slackened. With the end of T'ang, they cease. From T'ang onwards the Chinese potter no longer looks abroad for inspiration. Having absorbed what the Persian refugees had to offer, having dealt with the Graeco-Roman contributions of Buddhism, the Chinese have ceased to grow and begun to mature; and in maturity, as is well known, there is less change than in growth. The focal point of the empire has moved south, to more sober regions, further away from the ever-troublesome barbarians. The Chinese are embarked on that glorious era that will be described, three centuries later, by Marco Polo, who was dubbed a liar for his pains by a world not yet woken from its mediaeval sleep and unable to believe in the existence of such splendour elsewhere than in its own vague memories of Rome. Chinese products – Chinese ceramics – were to travel as far as Egypt, as far as Japan, to delight the princes of those lands. With their knowledge of the great achievements of T'ang – in painting, poetry, sculpture, conquest and belief – the princes of Samarra and Nara collected pottery also and stored it away. How much influence it exerted on those countries, especially on Japan, can be judged from the ceramic production of the succeeding age, the Sung, which the Japanese still seem to take as their model down to the present day.

Apart from the heritage of form which the Sung dynasty took over from T'ang, the later potters knew how to reap the full advantage from the interest and love for their ware that the T'ang artists had aroused. The industry was continued and enlarged (it was in Sung that for the first time ceramic wares came under imperial patronage), and manufacturing centres were established in many parts of the realm, each developing not only its own particular type of ware, porcelaneous

The medium.
Possibilities and triumphs

153

mostly, but restricting its gamut of forms and perfecting it. This specialisation, this concentration, probably provided the greatest single impulse in the whole ceramic industry of the Sung dynasty, accounting for a collection of works which surpassed any before it and has never been equalled since.

Though it has become a habit to regard the Sung dynasty as an odd hiatus in the typically Chinese continuity that joins T'ang to Ming (the dynasty which succeeds Sung), anyone free of this bias must recognise the T'ang origin of all the Sung forms and find it easy to explain the differences by examining the aesthetic and intellectual climate of that period, the mellowing that in all civilisations follows conquest and expansion. When the potters of the Ming dynasty reverted to pure T'ang forms for their inspiration, they responded to a general demand for a return to older styles typical of a conquering, militant era such as theirs. Having accomplished this deliberate archaicism they preposterously embellished the pure, original forms, and inaugurated the baroque of China, the beginning of her artistic decline.

If, as an enthusiast, one wonders why the products of the T'ang potter-sculptor have failed to find their proper place in the world's artistic pantheon one can only account for it by general fickleness of taste. However, it must be admitted that the efforts of the T'ang potter were far from uniformly successful, that the enormous production of a prosperous period bent on conforming to fashion could not but lead to mediocrity alongside excellence, slapdash effects alongside works carefully thought out. There is something in pottery as a medium that favours such a wide range of quality. Where stone and even clay is worked *in situ,* so to speak, where there is no opportunity to use moulds or to transfer the pieces from artist to craftsman to apprentice, such a wide range between excellence and mediocrity cannot occur. In the Graeco-Buddhist sculpture found in Persia and Afghanistan (another treasure quite as unappreciated as the one we are discussing)

XXX   JAR. *20 cm. high. The application of the generous green and caramel splashes over the white ground already dappled with blue is unique. Part of the green has turned into a silver and gold iridescence from its contact with acids in the earth. The ears are decorative vestiges of rabbits which have always been dear to the Chinese, probably because of the animal's pro-liferative talents, esteemed highly by those devoted ancestor-worshippers.*
                                 Collection Marchese G. F. Giaquili-Ferrini, Florence

XXXI   JAR. *18 cm. high. The glaze has been applied in several layers so as to obtain variations in the intensity of the colour. The vessel is lined with a fine straw-coloured glaze. An 'organic' quality is achieved by the play of fitted circles and spheres within its three-dimensional form, and makes of this a potter's bravura piece. The ghost was supposed to acquire sustenance from their effluvia rather than from the actual cereals and spirits that the vessels contained. Therefore it does seem logical that most of these jars should have been conceived without a cover.*
                                 Collection Marchese G. Litta-Modignani, Capalbio

there is no such wide disparity. The statuary, still anchored to its background, could not be obtained by moulds or by putting the pieces together by methods like those of present-day mass production. Yet to belittle the beautiful Chinese pieces because there are also mass-produced ones is patently unfair.

Finally a short description must be given not only of the techniques, simple enough, by which these T'ang objects were made, but also of the materials that were employed.

First, a brief explanation of the difference between earthenware, stoneware and porcelain – a difference which is still by no means fully understood. All three materials are derived from clay. They differ from one another in the amount of heat they are made to withstand in the oven and thus by the hardness they achieve – which is also conditioned by the *type* of clay that was originally used. Earthenware can stand only about 900° C. of heat and therefore after baking it remains porous, as the heat merely withdraws the water without fusing the clay. The glaze that is poured over the body before it is put into the kiln (silica, lime and potash or a lead oxide suspended in water) turns to a sort of glass. It is applied to earthenware objects mainly to keep them from leaking. Often, a 'slip' is applied over the body before the glaze is poured on, a mixture of lime and water which is seen through the glaze when this is transparent. Glazes containing lead oxide fuse in temperatures below 800° C. while other glazes, notably one made literally of rotten rock, discovered by the Chinese, require much higher temperatures for fusion. These are applied to bodies which, containing more refractory materials, stand higher temperatures and fuse, becoming stoneware. The glaze, not strictly speaking necessary, as stoneware is not porous, is merely an embellishment. When *kaolin* and *petuntze* are added to the clay, the firing temperature can go up to 1,450° C. and the result is porcelain. To be worthy of this name, the body must ring when struck, be white and allow the light through.

The soft earthenware commonly used by the T'ang potter – white, pink, grey or red after firing – first appears in the seventh century A.D. To begin with, this body is covered with a white slip and is painted in cold pigments. Soon after, however, colour becomes very popular: the bodies are covered with beautiful, shining glazes, though unglazed figures continue to be made – both freely painted after baking with the unfired pigments as before. How these glazes were suddenly called into existence and from where remains a mystery. One is tempted to go to

XXXII EWER. *11 cm. high. This exquisite shape, a telling example of Chinese transubstantiation of Persian silver shapes into pottery, is the most distinct forerunner in this T'ang collection of what is to come in Sung. To achieve the deep sapphire colour the potter has added some substance to his normal blue which alters its chemical structure when attacked by the acids in the earth. Some sections of the vessel, probably where it lay embedded in the damp clay of the grave, present iridescent discolourations which enhance the pure blue of the rest.*

Collection Dott. Gian Vincenzo Soro, Rome

the Han glazes already described, of course, but for this there is no valid evidence, even though both greens are procured from copper. Those who stubbornly refuse to grant the Chinese much inventive genius adduce the influence of the West even though no culture of the period has anything near the palette of the T'ang master – from oyster white through a rich cream, a golden yellow, a caramel, a blue of various hues to a near black (achieved by a too-intense green or a too-intense caramel). Whilst the colour obtained from cobalt, blue (a Mesopotamian invention), may indeed be of foreign origin, it is difficult to see how this can be true of the other glazes.

The manner in which the glazes were applied differs from the technique employed by the Han potters. While these poured the glaze on rather thickly, the T'ang artists favoured a thin glazing, probably because the finer texture of the baked clay of the body allowed this. Wherever only one colour was to be used, the method of application was dipping, that is to say, the vessel or figure was dipped into a vat of water wherein were suspended the minerals which upon firing procured the glaze and the colour. As to the method used where several colours were mingled, opinions differ. Some maintain that the oxides were applied dry on to the unglazed body and over these a transparent glaze was carefully poured so that after firing, the now coloured oxides could be seen through the glaze. Others maintain that the glazes were first stained and then applied side by side in the desired patterns. There are pieces where the second technique appears obvious, but in others it would seem impossible. Though the technique still used today by makers of cloisonné enamel suggests the second technique, it is probable that both were used, since both must inevitably have occurred to so perspicacious a person as the Chinese artisan.

Plates v, xiii, 98, 120

The technique of cloisonné just mentioned (where thickly suspended enamel colours are placed inside *cloisons* or sections confined by metal ridges) leads us to the incised patterns, mostly on plates, where the colours were, to some extent at least, prevented from running into each other by the grooves which formed the design. Often these designs are rather rigidly stylised and this has caused some experts to believe that they do not belong to the T'ang era with its freedom of design even though they are ready to accept the notion of Persian influence – of which this rigidity is typical – in other fields.

While the vessels were, of course, turned on the potters' wheel, the modelling

XXXIII *GUARDIAN WARRIOR. 52½ cm. high. This large and fine figure is of great interest to the student of foreign influences in Chinese art because its features are so obviously inspired by Graeco-Buddhist sculpture of Northern India, Afghanistan and Persia. The armour worn is in the Persian tradition, but the dramatic attitude is purely Chinese, current to this day in Chinese classical opera. The delicate but forceful decoration in unfired pigments over the glaze, the buff clay of the body and the cream-yellowish hue of the glaze are associated with the production of the Sui or early T'ang periods.* Royal Ontario Museum, Toronto

Plates 43, 75 of the sculpture was done in three ways: by sticking together moulds with a brief attempt to hide the joins; by using moulds but carefully eliminating all indications that could reveal this method, and finally finishing by hand; by pure modelling. The meagre importance of the first two is fairly self-evident, but it is amazing that the third group should have been so little appreciated.

Let us, while we are considering the importance of this artistic effort, look at it for an instant in the context of its epoch, in comparison with the other artistic manifestations of T'ang. It is clear that this more than any other brims over with originality, with a clear departure from the accepted. In comparison with the stone sculptures of the great Buddhist era the clay pieces from the tombs possess a tremendous dynamism, a movement in all directions. Unlike his stone-mason colleague, the T'ang potter is concerned with movement, with diversity, with the creation of novelty. It is as though the material in which the tomb figures are made, the very clay which the sculptor has so happily discovered, were suddenly liberating him from the static qualities of the Buddhist canons which the medium of stone had encouraged.

It is for us, standing apart and looking back, with the burden of our cumulative experience, to judge how successful he has been. But we are accustomed to divide up art into impressionism and expressionism, naturalism and the abstract – and when we are looking for one, we refuse to find the other. Thus we are prevented from recognising the Chinese potter's success by self-imposed blinkers which do not allow impressionism and expressionism to be seen together, let alone merge or mingle.

But if they were allowed to, if they could? With great and equal power, so that one did not rule out the other? With such passionate devotion to nature as to remain always this side of the preposterous? Could we not then say that the creation of the T'ang potter is – as far as we with our cumulative experience over the centuries can judge – perfect within its own limits?

Even those who refuse to see the sensitive play of abstract surfaces in a fine T'ang horse must admit that there is no more felicitous abstraction than a T'ang vessel – that there is no happier marriage of form and decoration than in for example the striate jar of Plate XXVIII.

XXXIV AMPHORA. *32 cm. high. The handles are formed by two stylized dragons biting the rim; they are more frequent in the porcelain of the period, the Shing Yao, in which the fine ewer on plate XIX was turned. In that material, the neck becomes longer and the shoulders drop to form a more egg-like body. Except for the dragons, this could be a Graeco-Roman specimen, though the idea of leaving the glaze so short of the base and allowing it to stop so irregularly is again quite Chinese – a desire to entrust the finish to nature.* Collection Mr Samuel Lee, Tokyo

97   AGNI, the Indian god of fire. 87½ cm. high. Unglazed pottery with traces of painting in pigments. This foreign deity was adopted to keep evil influences away by its fierceness. *Seattle Art Museum.*

98   JAR WITH COVER. 39¼ cm. high. Three colour glazes over an etched design. The unusual cover turns one's thoughts to the Near East. *Victoria and Albert Museum, London.*

99   RHYTON CUP. 8¾ cm. high. Three colour glazes over a white body. The Graeco-Roman influence is apparent, though this piece may well be the pottery copy of a silver specimen from Persia. *Royal Ontario Museum, Toronto.*

100   JAR WITH COVER. 19¼ cm. high. Thin cream glaze over a white body. *Victoria and Albert Museum, London.*

101   VASE WITH COVER. 26¼ cm. high. Three colour glazes over a white body. *Victoria and Albert Museum, London.*

102   JAR WITH COVER. 16 cm. high. White glaze with green dabs over a white body. *Collection Marchese G. Litta-Modignani, Capalbio.*

103   SMALL COVERED TRIPOD. 7½ cm. high. Glazed in deep caramel, ivory and moss green over a pinkish body. The cover, mottled green on caramel. *Collection Marchese G. Litta-Modignani, Capalbio.*

104   GROOM. Caramel and cream glazes over a white body, face and hands unglazed. The figure has been sawn across to lessen the hazards of unlawful transportation from the burial sites. *Victoria and Albert Museum, London.*

105   EWER. 16 cm. high. White porcelain, *Shing Yao.* The lion biting the rim is treated in the impressionistic manner in which T'ang and Sung potters have done the innumerable miniature *Ming Chi* which some believe were meant to delight departed children. *Collection Dott. Gian Vincenzo Soro, Rome.*

106 PILGRIM BOTTLE. 12½ cm. high. Green glaze over a white body. This very early Asiatic shape must have been made by the same workshop as the ewer in Plate 109, for the dancing boys are identical. *Royal Ontario Museum, Toronto.*

107 JAR WITH COVER. 23¾ cm. high. Cream blossoms on a green ground, the edges of the cream diagonal stripes outlined in blue and caramel glazes. The body a pinkish white. *British Museum, London.*

108 Detail of Plate 109.

109 EWER. 25 cm. high. Three colour glazes over the whole body and relief decoration. The first impression is one of pure Greek influence. But, apart from the Hellenistic flower-and-fruit decoration, the shape of the vessel is Sassanian Persian, and the dancing figure is a youth wearing the Indian dhoti and waving a scarf – not like a Greek nymph, but in the traditional manner of a tree-sprite often found in Indian art. *Royal Ontario Museum, Toronto.*

110 SMALL VASE AND BOWL. 8½ and 3¾ cm. high. Three colour glazes (cream, caramel and green) over a pinkish-white body.

111 TRIPOD JAR. 16½ cm. high. Three colour glazes over a white body and applied medallions. The lipped version of this vessel is the more common. *Royal Ontario Museum, Toronto.*

112 EWER. 21½ cm. high. Green glaze over a white body. This Picasso-like shape was inspired by Caucasian bronzes, the larger bird's head being of a type frequently found in Central Asiatic decoration. *Royal Ontario Museum, Toronto.*

113 EWER. 32 cm. high. Creamy-white glaze over a white earthenware body. While the dragon head on the handle is purely Chinese, the applied decorations are of Persian derivation (See Plate 25). *Seattle Art Museum.*

114 EWER. 32 cm. high. Light caramel and blue glazes over a buff body. This side depicts a dancing phoenix, a popular representation in T'ang art; the other, a galloping Parthian horseman turning in the saddle and shooting an arrow – the 'Parthian shot'. The pearl which the bird bears in its beak is probably a Buddhist emblem. *T. Y. King, Jr, Hongkong.*

115 TRIPOD JAR. 13¾ cm. high. Three colour glazes over a white body and applied medallions imitating silver repoussé work. *Royal Ontario Museum, Toronto.*

116 JAR. 22 cm. high. *Shing Yao* porcelain. White glaze. A perfect example of the T'ang potter's success in transferring his 'shape-consciousness' to the new material, porcelain. *Seattle Art Museum, Margaret E. Fuller Purchase Fund, Seattle.*

117 VASE. 37½ cm. high. *Shing Yao* porcelain. Cream glaze. This fine shape is obviously inspired by a leather pilgrim bottle. The thongs running down the belly, a vestige from its leather prototype, have become a most effective decorative element. *Royal Ontario Museum, Toronto.*

118 JAR. 13 cm. high. The applied medallions in leaf and frog form are again of Persian inspiration, copies of similar silver work which Sassanian refugees were chasing in T'ang China. Three colour glazes over a pinkish-white body. *Collection Marchese G. Litta-Modignani, Capalbio.*

119 JAR. 19 cm. high. Three colour glazes over applied medallions on a white body. The geometric pattern is unusual. *Royal Ontario Museum, Toronto.*

120 PILLOW. 16½ cm. high. Green, cream and caramel glazes over an incised pattern of strong Persian influence. *Seattle Art Museum.*

98

99

100

101

102

103

104

105

106

107

108

110

111

114

115

116

117

118

119

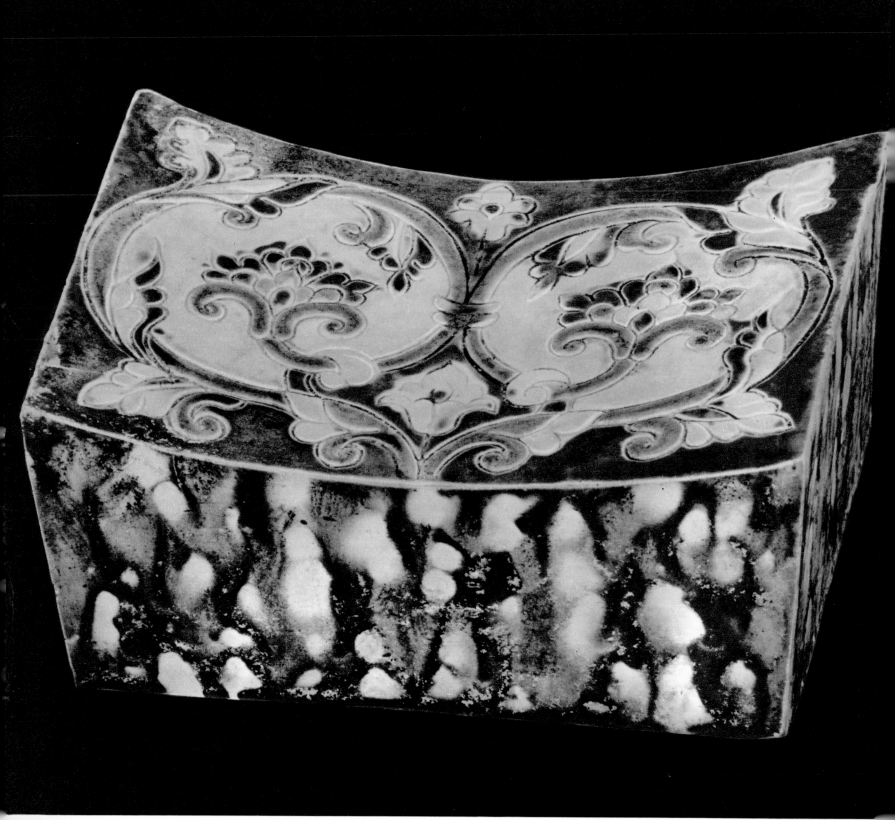

120

Bibliography
List of Colour Plates
Index

Bibliography

DEXEL, TH.: *Die Formen chinesischer Keramik*, Tübingen, 1955

HONEY, W. B.: *The Ceramic Art of China and other Countries of the Far East*, London, 1954

GRAY, B.: *Early Chinese Pottery and Porcelain*, London, 1953

GROUSSET, R.: *La Chine et son Art*, Paris, 1951

FEDERSEN, M.: *Chinesisches Kunstgewerbe*, Berlin, 1939

COHN, W.: *Chinese Art*, London, 1930

HENTZE, C.: *Chinese Tomb Figures*, London, 1928

SALMONY, A.: *Chinesische Plastik*, Berlin, 1925

SCHMIDT, R.: *Chinesische Keramik von der Han-Zeit bis zum XIX Jahrhundert*, Frankfurt, 1924

HETHERINGTON, A. L.: *The Art of the Chinese Potter*, London, 1922

STEIN, SIR A.: *The Thousand Buddhas*, London, 1921

DORE, H., S. J.: *Recherches sur les Superstitions en Chine*, Shanghai, 1919

GRANET, M.: *La Religion des Chinois*, Paris, 1919

HOBSON, R. L.: *Chinese Pottery and Porcelain*, London, 1915

LAUFER, B.: *Chinese Clay Figures*, Chicago, 1914

GROOT, J. M. DE: *The Religious System of China*, Leyden, 1912

MAHLER, J. G.: *The Westerners among the Figurines of the T'ang Dynasty of China*, Rome, 1959

List of Colour Plates

Index   *Including references to colour and black and white plates*

INVENTORY 74

SPRING 77

INVENTORY 1983

INVENTORY 74